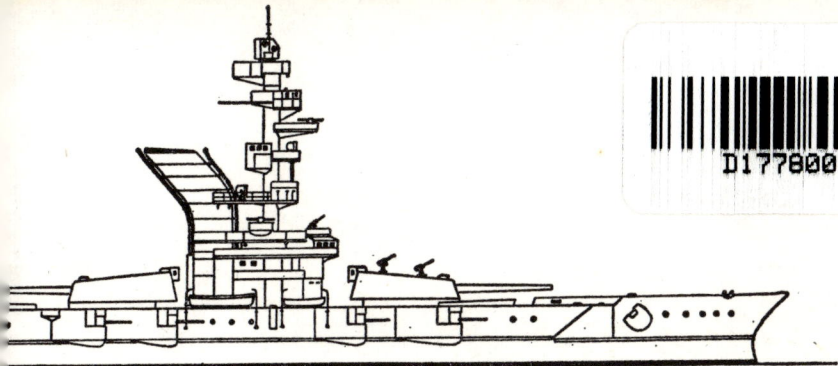

D1778001

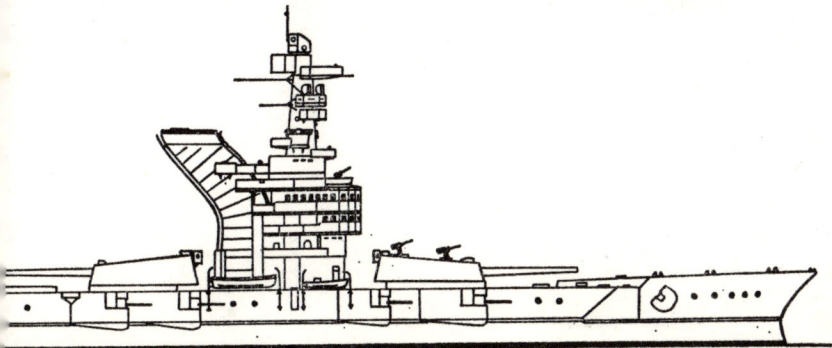

© Jürg Meister, 1972

SBN 356 03043 1

First published in 1972 by
Macdonald & Co. (Publishers) Ltd.,
49 Poland Street, London, W.1
Made and printed in Great Britain by
Hazell, Watson and Viney Ltd.,
Aylesbury, Bucks

FOREWORD

Since 1945 all the major belligerents who were involved in the Second World War, with the exception of the Soviet Union and Communist-bloc countries, have published comprehensive and objective official histories about naval operations and the losses incurred.

Although many books and articles mainly dealing with the naval war have been published in the Soviet Union, not one of them gives a complete and detached account of Soviet or enemy naval losses or a complete list of vessels which composed the wartime Soviet Navy. In addition, these biased accounts understate Soviet losses and grossly inflate the number of enemy vessels claimed sunk. They are in no sense histories but sheer propaganda, and were initially quoted as authoritative versions in Western publications until laborious research in the post-war years showed them to be utterly false.

The scope of these four volumes on the Soviet Navy is to give an outline of its material strength and composition and the losses sustained over the period of hostilities. Although the author has spent over 20 years collecting information to this end many gaps still exist as to the identity and fate of some minor warships and auxiliary vessels. Owing to the biased attitude of the Soviet authorities it is now unlikely that many of these omissions will ever be resolved.

Printed sources referred to in assembling this information includes pre-war intelligence contained in the German Admiralty handbook on the Soviet Navy and similar Western publications (full of many errors and omissions); and also original documents which, from June 1941 onwards, fell into German hands, like lists of warships captured at Libau (Liepaja), Reval (Tallinn), Nikolaiev, and Sevastopol, statements obtained from prisoners-of-war, and documents found on wrecked warships.

Among these were the official silhouette handbook of the vessels of the Baltic Fleet in 1939, numerous reports about technical shortcomings of individual vessels, the Soviet Register of Merchant Ships 1938–39, and many other items. Numerous German aerial photographs provided verification of the various warships under construction in the Baltic and Black Sea between 1941–42, while the German Admiralty Handbook 1944 (based on captured documents and therefore far more reliable) and the American Office of Naval Information (ONI) publications up to 1947 were of great assistance.

The evaluation of several hundred Soviet naval books and articles yielded more confusion than precision. Very few (if any) Soviet authors appear to have access to all documents, and through repeated errors by Soviet historians the true facts have been obscured. Even today few Soviet naval personnel have some knowledge of the composition of their own fleet much less that of the whole Soviet Navy, and the same situation prevailed during the war years.

Soviet naval books always mitigate information concerning losses by being vague and incomplete. One book will merely state that an unnamed minesweeper was lost on a certain date in the Arctic and give no other details; another will give the name and nothing else; while a third will simply provide the circumstances which occasioned the loss. From all three the complete picture—name of vessel and cause, location, and date of loss—can be built-up together with that available in German documents. One fact that persistently evades research in this direction is uncovering the former mercantile name when the vessel concerned is an auxiliary warship. In the Soviet Union information on naval losses sustained during the Second World War is still classified because of the fear that such information would tarnish the myth of Soviet naval impregnability. Any historian knows that the success, or failure, of an operation is not measured solely in terms of the losses incurred but whether the losses were reasonable in attaining the particular objective.

Another frequently quoted Soviet source is the *Spravochnik Korabelnovo Sostava Voenno-Morskikh Sil* published in 1944. This naval handbook copied the text of the 1943 issue of Jane's *Fighting Ships* for foreign navies, while only one ship of each class is mentioned for the section on the Soviet Navy. Most of the particulars quoted are deliberately false and some of the photographs—all of outstandingly poor quality—do not correspond to the text. The Soviet authorities published this book in order to feed their erstwhile Allies false information about the Soviet Navy, and from this wholly unreliable source stem many of the errors found in post-war Western naval reference books up to 1960.

The fact that most of the German naval archives fell into British hands explains up to a point the ridiculous claims of the Soviet Navy on the losses they inflicted on Axis naval forces. Rather than take advantage of Western sources compiled from the original German documents Soviet claims continue to be based on their wartime bulletins which contain many inaccuracies with regards to ship names and ship types.

Up to 1956 Soviet naval books were of no serious value, but this was followed by a short period of semi-enlightenment when some half-truths could be admitted. From 1962, however, the hard propaganda line has re-asserted itself and the illusion is still proffered that it was the Soviet Navy that beat the German and Japanese navies single-handed. The official line is still that 4 million Finns deliberately provoked 200 million Russians in 1939; and when discussing the war against Japan no mention is made of the fact that by the time the Soviet Union intervened—in August 1945—all the major Japanese warships had been either sunk or damaged by the United States Navy, or that the few surviving units were immobilised as fuel stocks had been exhausted.

There is only one thing of a poorer quality than Soviet naval publications and that is Soviet naval photographs, many of which have been retouched very clumsily. Where no other illustration is available they have been used of necessity and are credited U.S.S.R.; while most of the remaining photographs are from the author's own collection and are credited J.M. The negatives of the latter were sold in 1966 to the *Bibliothek für Zeitgeschichte* (BfZ), Stuttgart, whose director—Dr. J. Rohwer—kindly helped and advised on many issues.

The author would also like to acknowledge the invaluable assistance of the late Kurt von Nottbeck, a former Imperial Russian naval officer who served for some time with the Estonian and German Navies; Pierre Warneck, a former Imperial Russian naval cadet, whose first-hand knowledge of Czarist-built ships was of great help; Siegfried Breyer for the many excellent drawings which are reproduced in these volumes; Lt. Cdr. R. C. Dulin, U.S.N. who kindly provided the interesting data on the Soviet battleships that were projected between 1936–41 from his forthcoming book on dreadnought-type battleships, Rear Admiral E. M. Eller, U.S. Navy (ret.), Director of Naval History, Dept. of the Navy; Capt. R. Steen Steensen, R.D.N. (ret.); Monsieur H. Le Masson; Dott. A. Fraccaroli and Mijnher L. L. von Münching.

The author is particularly indebted to Rolf Erikson, Phoenix, U.S.A. whose painstaking research from a wide variety of sources makes him one of the foremost authorities on Soviet Naval history between 1918–45. Without his generous help this series of books on the Soviet Navy could not have been produced. Finally, many private individuals and a few official bodies who prefer to remain anonymous made important contributions which were much appreciated.

The author's intention was not to vilify the Soviet Navy but to provide as clear and accurate a picture as possible not only of its failures and shortcomings but also of the undeniable effort and sacrifice made during the first 28 years of its existence. One strange fact emerged, namely that the Soviet Navy was—and still is—either much underestimated or overestimated by the rest of the world.

Between 1945 and the present date the Free World, with the exception of the United States, helped the Soviet Union in building a new navy by providing technical assistance and undertaking merchant ship orders so leaving Soviet yards free for warship construction. In tonnage, the Soviet Navy now ranks second in the world, but size is not everything. The Russian Navy in 1904, and the Soviet Navy in 1939–40 and 1941–45, was numerically stronger than opposing naval forces and yet failed to exercise a dominating influence. The scope of this work is to accord to the Soviet Navy its due place for its role in the Second World War.

Zürich, 1971. J.M.

INTRODUCTION

This first of several volumes dealing with the vessels of the Soviet Navy during the Second World War lists the battleships, battlecruisers, aircraft- and seaplane carriers, heavy and light cruisers, flotilla leaders, destroyers, and torpedo boats (the later vessels of this type were classed as *storoshevoi korably*, literally guard ships) that were in service, building, or projected over this period; and may be termed the major surface units of the Soviet Fleet.

Gunboats, minelayers and minesweepers, patrol vessels and submarine chasers, motor launches, and armoured motor gunboats will form a second volume containing light surface forces. The third volume will embrace submarines and motor torpedo boats; while the numerous minor vessels attached to lake and river flotillas, together with sea-going auxiliaries, training ships, surveying vessels, landing craft, icebreakers, transports, and other miscellaneous craft will be listed in a final volume.

The Soviet Navy was composed of warships derived from five different sources, viz:

(a) former Imperial Navy vessels completed before October 1917;
(b) former Imperial Navy vessels laid down before 1917 and completed by the Soviet Navy after long delays;
(c) vessels built between 1928–45 by the Soviet Navy;
(d) vessels transferred from the American and British navies under Lend/Lease between 1942–45; and
(e) former Bulgarian, Rumanian, and Finnish vessels taken over in 1944.

Major warships belonging to the former Imperial Navy comprised three battleships, two cruisers, eleven old destroyers, and some old torpedo boats; while three cruisers and six destroyers laid down before 1917 were completed between 1925–32. In 1941 all these vessels were over 25 years old and of little fighting value.

7

According to an official—but incomplete and deliberately vague—Soviet statement five hundred and thirty-three warships (excluding boats) were laid down between 1928–41, and these probably included:

2	battleships*	36	escort vessels
2	battlecruisers*	2	netlayers
18	cruisers**	10	river monitors
82	flotilla leaders and destroyers	9	river gunboats
297	submarines	17	large submarine chasers
55	minesweepers	2	unidentified vessels

However, not all the vessels laid down were completed, as will be seen by an examination of the following pages. During the war Soviet yards delivered two cruisers, twenty-five destroyers, escorts and minesweepers, fifty-two submarines—all of which were laid down before 22/6/41—as well as 972 assorted boats (MTB, AMGB, minesweeping launches and subchasers) most of which were laid down during the war.

Among the major Lend/Lease vessels were one old British battleship, one old American cruiser, nine old American destroyers, and four British submarines. When the war in the Black Sea was over the Soviet Navy seized at Constanta four Rumanian destroyers which did not take an active role for the remainder of the war.

* Neither was ever completed.
** Of these only 6 were commissioned up to 1945, and 5 more later, while the construction of the remaining 7 had to be cancelled.

The composition of the major surface vessels in service with the seagoing Soviet Navy 1941–45 was as follows:

	Czarist-built	Soviet-built	Foreign-built or Lend/Lease	Captured	Total
Battleships	3	—	1	—	4
Battlecruisers	—	—	—	—	—
Heavy cruisers	—	—	1[1]	—	1
Medium cruisers	1[2]	6	—	—	7
Light cruisers	4[3]	—	1[4]	—	5
Flotilla leaders	—	6	1[5]	—	7
Destroyers	17[6]	48	9	4	78
Torpedo boats and guard ships	2	18+7[7]	2[8]	6	28

The distribution of the major surface vessels in commission by 22/6/41 was as follows:

	Baltic	Arctic	Far East	Black Sea	Total
Battleships	2	—	—	1	3
Heavy cruisers	1[1]	—	—	—	1
Medium cruisers	2	—	—	3	5
Light cruisers	1	—	—	3	4
Flotilla leaders	2	—	2	3	7
Modern destroyers	12[9]	5[9]	10	8[9]	35
Old destroyers	7	3	2	5	17
Torpedo boats and guard ships	9	3	6+2[7]	2	22

At the close of the war the distribution of major surface vessels were as follows, taking into account war losses, Lend/Lease deliveries, captured vessels, and war construction:

	Baltic	Arctic	Far East	Black Sea	Total
Battleships	1	1	—	1	3
Heavy cruisers	1[1]	—	—	—	1
Medium cruisers	2	—	2[11]	3	7
Light cruisers	1[12]	1[4]	—	1	3
Flotilla leaders	2	1	1	—	4
Modern destroyers commissioned before 22/6/41	5	5	8	3	21
Modern destroyers commissioned after 22/6/41	5[11]	—	2[11]	1[11]	8
Lend/Lease destroyers	—	8[10]	—	—	8
Old destroyers	—	3	2	2	7
Captured destroyers	—	—	—	4	4
Torpedo boats and guard ships completed before 1942	3	—	6+2[8]	2	13
Torpedo boats and guard ships completed after 1942 excluding Lend/Lease frigates	5(?)	—	2(?)	—	7
Captured torpedo boats	—	—	—	6	6

[1] Incomplete ex-German unit used as a floating battery 1941–45; [2] laid down as light cruiser for the Imperial Navy and completed as medium cruiser for Soviet Navy; [3] two old Czarist-built units of no fighting value and two units laid down by the Imperial Navy and completed by the Soviet Navy; [4] Lend/Lease (ex-USN); [5] Italian-built *Tashkent* completed in 1939; [6] eleven of these units were already in service with the Imperial Navy and six under construction were completed by the Soviet Navy; [7] "Bird" class escorts, some completed but not employed during the war; [8] Italian-built patrol vessels *Kirov* and *Dzerzhinski* completed for the NKVD Sea Frontier Guard and commissioned as naval escorts during the war; [9] some units were not completed until after the outbreak of war; [10] Lend/Lease vessels; [11] laid down before 1941 and completed during the war; [12] *Avrora* sunk in shallow water and salved post-war.

Note: In Soviet statistics the very old light cruisers *Avrora* and *Komintern* were listed as training vessels, not cruisers.

When considering the activities of the Soviet Navy between 1939–45 it is necessary to distinguish between six distinct phases:

(a) the Soviet invasion of Poland in 1939 with no cost to the Soviet Navy other than that of an old collier which they scuttled so that the false charge of piracy could be levelled against the Polish Navy;

(b) the Soviet war with Finland in 1939–40 which cost the Soviet Navy at least one submarine, one armed tug, and one motor launch sunk, and several other major surface units damaged;

(c) the Soviet annexation of the Baltic states of Esthonia, Latvia, and Lithuania in 1940 and the acquisition of the small naval force possessed by each;

(d) the Soviet war with Germany between 1941–45 which resulted in the Soviet Navy losing about half their pre-war forces;

(e) Soviet participation in the British invasion of Iran in 1941 which enabled the Soviet Caspian Flotilla to seize any Iranian ship operated on that inland sea; and

(f) the belated Soviet participation in the war against Japan in 1945 which nevertheless incurred some loss of minesweepers, motor launches, and motor torpedo boats, although the bulk of the Soviet Pacific (Far East) Fleet—two cruisers, ten destroyers, and seventy-eight submarines—was not involved.

In the 1939–40 war with Finland the Soviet Baltic and Arctic fleets and the Lake Ladoga flotilla, although about ten times stronger than the Finnish Navy, were unable to exercise a blockade, destroy coastal fortifications, or land troops (except where Finnish forces had been withdrawn), and their influence on the conflict was practically nil. Successes at sea were equally sparing: the Finnish auxiliary patrol vessel *Aura*, five Finnish and three neutral merchant ships were sunk, and one small Finnish merchant ship captured.

In the war with Germany the Soviet Navy lost the following major surface units between 1941–45: one battleship, three old cruisers (one salved post-war), three flotilla leaders, twenty modern and ten old destroyers, and at least four modern torpedo boats. These losses were heavy enough, but when it is taken into account that not one enemy war- or merchant ship was sunk by major Soviet surface forces, then the performance of the Soviet Navy was beggarly in the extreme.

The strategic influence of a navy in war can of course not be measured solely by the losses suffered or inflicted. In two World Wars the Royal Navy lost more surface warships than the German Navy, but was nevertheless able to maintain a blockade which proved decisive. The Soviet Navy did also lose far more warships than the Axis-powers, but failed to exercise any notable strategic influence upon the conduct of the war on sea and land in the East. The war against Germany was won by the Soviet Army which captured all German-held ports from the landside.

To the number of Soviet major surface units lost in action must be added those ships which, building in 1941, fell incomplete into German hands or whose construction had to be abandoned. These include two battleships, two battlecruisers, seven cruisers, four flotilla leaders, and several destroyers. Of the major surface units building in 1941 only one destroyer was completed in the Arctic and another in the Black Sea in 1943, while two cruisers and a few destroyers were completed in Far East yards. This meant that only about 20% of the cruisers, and 30% of the destroyers, that were under construction in 1941 were completed, and no major surface units at all were laid down during the war.

The cause of loss of major surface units is shown in the following summary:

	Gunfire	Bombed	Mined	Torpedoed	Miscellaneous causes	Total
Battleships	—	1	—	—	—	1
Cruisers	—	3	—	—	—	3
Flotilla leaders	—	2	1	—	—	3
Modern destroyers	—	10	8	1	1	20
Old destroyers	—	4	5	—	1	10
Torpedo boats and guard ships	—	2	3	—	—	5

Note: one of the modern destroyers listed as mined may have been torpedoed by a submarine, and some of the others had first incurred bomb or torpedo damage.

During the whole war, and in all theatres, Soviet major surface vessels were never engaged in surface actions with similar German, Finnish or Rumanian naval forces. Even when Soviet major surface forces, mostly destroyers, met on a few occasions much inferior Axis forces, they always broke off the engagement after a few salvoes. Notwithstanding the heavy Soviet losses incurred, the Soviet major surface naval forces were almost always superior to the Axis forces, especially in the Black Sea, where the bulk of the Axis naval strength consisted of 2 modern and 2 old Rumanian destroyers, while the Soviets could almost always muster one battleship, at least two or three cruisers and never less than six destroyers. In the Baltic in 1942 and 1943 the blockade of the Gulf of Finland was maintained by Finnish and German light forces (minesweepers, subchasers, gunboats and auxiliaries) supported by one Finnish coast defence vessel and a few German coasters converted into auxiliary gunboats armed with 6-inch guns. The few raids the Soviet Navy attempted with major surface forces against Axis shipping in the Baltic in 1941 and the Black Sea in 1941–1942–1943 proved costly failures and were given up after the loss of a flotilla leader and two destroyers on the 6/10/43 off the Crimean coast.

(Above) The MARAT *before the war*

[JM/BfZ

(Left) The old protected cruiser AVRORA *on the River Neva in April 1918*

USSR

(Left) The MARAT *sunk in shallow water at Kronstadt late in September 1941 after being hit by German dive bombers*

(Right) A wartime view of the SEVASTOPOL *(ex-*PARIZHSKAYA KOMMUNA*). Note additional A.A. guns*
[JM/BfZ

There are many reasons to account for the complete lack of success of the Soviet Navy's major surface warships. The twenty-five Czarist-built battleships, cruisers and destroyers still in service in 1941 were obsolescent, but so were most of the Finnish, Rumanian and German warships employed in the East. The more modern Soviet warships were subject to frequent breakdowns and some were commissioned with incomplete armament and only partially trained crews. The maintenance of the warships which had survived the various retreats and evacuations in the Baltic in 1941 and the Black Sea in 1942 proved very difficult, as Leningrad was blockaded and besieged until 1944, while the Caucasian ports which remained in Soviet hands lacked the repair facilities lost at Nikolaiev, Sevastopol and Novorossisk. The use of Soviet naval crews for fighting ashore—a task which they undertook with great gallantry—resulted not only in heavy losses, but also in additional lack of sea-training, which was already in general on a low level.

The major factor, however, was the bad quality of the officer corps, which was more politically reliable than professionally capable. Only very few former Imperial Navy officers had survived all the purges and remained in active service by 1941. Most of the high-ranking officers in 1941 were former petty-officers or seamen, their political zeal compensating their lack of military instruction. The ruthless purges Stalin had undertaken in 1937–1939 had not spared the Soviet Navy, and numerous high-ranking Soviet naval officers had been executed for no other reason than disapproving of Stalin's ideas about building an ocean-going navy.

Among the high-ranking officers executed as a result of pre-war purges were Mukklevich, Orlov, Ludri, Zivkov, Kozhanov, Dushenov, Kadatskii-Rudnev, Alexsandrov, Stashevitshy, Petrov, Jerve, Frinovskyj, Dybenko, Antonov-Ovseyenko Zof, and Smirnov: all of whom had served as C-in-C's of the various Soviet fleets, senior officers of squadrons and flotillas, or instructors at the Naval War School. The staff officer corps was also badly instructed, and only among the junior officers were there some with an adequate professional background. The general lack of initiative inherent to the Russian character combined with the Communist doctrine of strict adherence to the party line prevented even the few gifted officers from taking any decision which could be interpreted as politically suspect. Only operations ordered from the Supreme Command were carried out with determination and without regard to casualties.

The lack of seamanship, which had hampered the Imperial Navy during the era of sail, was of less importance during the Second World War. However, when on one occasion a destroyer of the Arctic fleet kept at sea for three consecutive days this "outstanding feat" was much publicised. The Royal Navy was particularly bitter about the lack of co-operation in escorting Northern convoys, and carried out this arduous duty practically unaided and at considerable cost. The Soviet forces, however, had a good knowledge of the Arctic and their equipment for this area was basic but efficient.

The technical equipment of the Soviet Navy did not match the standards of Western navies. Although the new 3·9-inch (100 mm.) and 5·1-inch (130 mm.) guns were good, fire control was poor and seldom on target, while right up to the end of hostilities quite inadequate A.A. armaments were shipped. Torpedoes were of indifferent quality and lacked any refinements such as acoustic or magnetic pistols or electric propulsion. Soviet A/S equipment and tactics were even worse, and there was a complete absence of asdic or any efficient under-water listening apparatus, and similar conditions prevailed in the submarine arm. Even in mine warfare—the only branch of naval warfare in which they enjoyed a high reputation—the Soviet Navy was inept, and far from maintaining the tradition established under the Czarist regime with either mining and minesweeping. The development of radar had been completely overlooked and was introduced to the Soviet Navy on vessels supplied on Lend/Lease.

Naval equipment provided under Lend/Lease included radar, asdic, mines, torpedoes, ammunition, and diesel engines. The Soviet Navy, however, rejected the advice of the Royal Navy on how to instal and operate this equipment, and such was their mistrust that they would even provide plans of their destroyers so that they could be instructed exactly where to instal asdic domes. Consequently, the performance of asdic was below standard and A/S efficiency was impaired.

Therefore, while the under-trained Soviet sailor was more in his element fighting ashore, the officers and petty officers showed themselves to be technically and tactically inferior to their Western allies and Axis enemies. Nor were they helped by a High Command that lacked strategic naval insight. The impact of the Soviet Navy on the high seas was negligible, but their ships displayed considerable tenacity when employed as a "fortress fleet" and during some amphibious operations. This, however, was not the proper role for a large fleet of surface vessels which at almost any time in every theatre enjoyed a considerable margin of superiority over enemy naval forces.

With regard to the naming of Soviet warships up to 1943 the battleships commemorated the October Revolution and the 1871 Commune of Paris and another the Swiss-born revolutionary Jean-Paul Marat (1743–1793), but in 1943 two of them reverted to their former traditional names of *Sevastopol* and *Petropavlovsk*. The old destroyers bore the names of leading Communists despite the fact that *Karl Marx, Karl Liebknecht, Friedrich Engels*, and *Rosa Luxembourg* were Germans; but the names of the many foreigners who had served the former Imperial Navy were strictly excluded.

Cruisers were named after prominent Soviet party members, flotilla leaders after large towns, mine-layers and netlayers after rivers and lakes, while modern destroyers perpetuated traditional Imperial Navy names like Bold, Courageous, Fast, etc. Minesweepers of the "Tral" class carried names related to weapons, navigational equipment, and equipment in use on warships; and guard ships were all named after meteorological phenomena such as Storm, Squall, Blizzard, Tempest, etc.

A bewildering aspect of Soviet naval history is the frequent changes of names that accompanied any fresh political outlook. Thus the cruiser *Molotov*, and other vessels were suddenly renamed in 1957 when these political figures were discredited. In books published after this date the reader is regaled with the war-time activities of the cruiser *Slava*, etc., but no mention is ever made of their former names and the resulting confusion is easily imagined.

BATTLESHIPS

During the Russo-Japanese War 1904–05 the Imperial Russian Navy lost fourteen sea-going and three coast defence battleships, some of which were captured by the Japanese. At the close of the war battleship strength was reduced to nine units in the Black Sea (some of which were very old), one interned at Kiatschou, and one under construction in the Baltic.

In 1907 two 17,400-ton pre-dreadnought battleships armed with four 12-inch (305 mm.) and fourteen 8-inch (203 mm.) were completed in the Baltic.

The construction of the first Russian dreadnoughts was put out to both foreign and local tenders, and of the fifty-one received ten were chosen for final selection (including one Russian). The contract was to be awarded to Blohm & Voss, Hamburg, when the Government intervened and stipulated that they had to be built in Russian yards. The Naval Staff therefore produced a fresh design, largely based on that of Cuniberti, and incorporated some of the interesting features from the other plans submitted.

The final result was a far from happy combination, and although the vessels (known as Gangut class) were well-armed and faster than most contemporaries, their protection was noticeably weaker, they lacked constructional strength, and they were poorly ventilated. As they took five/seven years to build, by the time they were completed they were outclassed. Their 12-inch guns had a rate of fire of $1\frac{1}{2}$–2 rounds/min but the hull could not withstand a full broadside.

During the First World War the Imperial Navy lost the pre-dreadnought *Slava* and the dreadnought *Imperatritsa Maria*, and purchased two former Russian pre-dreadnoughts from Japan; but one of the latter—the *Peresviet*—was mined and lost en-route to the Arctic. All remaining old battleships—one in the Arctic, four in the Baltic, and six in the Black Sea—were damaged during the ensuing Civil War, and two taken over by White Russian forces in Sevastopol could only be employed as floating batteries as their machinery had been wrecked by the British to prevent their use by Red Russian forces. After the Civil War the Soviet Navy scrapped all pre-dreadnought battleships remaining in their hands, and were left with four damaged dreadnoughts in the Baltic and one fast battleship under construction in the Black Sea.

Authorised in 1914, the fast battleship *Nikolai I* had a displacement of 27,627 tons, dimensions of 597 × 94½ × 29½ feet (182 × 28·83 × 9 m.), a better protection than the dreadnoughts, and was to be armed with twelve 12-inch (305 mm.) and twenty 5-inch (127 mm.) guns. Launched on 18/10/16, she was renamed *Demokratiya* in 1917, and remained at Nikolaiev throughout the Civil War. The Soviet Navy was unable to complete her and she was scrapped after 1922.

The fate of the seven dreadnought battleships laid down before the First World War is as follows:

Name	Builder	Laid down	Launched	Completed
Poltava	Admiralty Yard (St. Petersburg)	13.7.09	10.7.11	17.12.14

Damaged during the Civil War and later cannibalised for spares. Never went to sea again after spring 1918, and report that she was renamed *Frunze* unsubstantiated and unlikely. Hulk towed to Kronstadt in 1941 and expended as a blockship. Scrapped 1956.

Name	Builder	Laid down	Launched	Completed
Gangut	Admiralty Yard (St. Petersburg)	13.7.09	7.10.11	5.1.15

Renamed *Oktyabrskaya Revolutsia* on 7/7/25 and recommissioned in 8/26; decommissioned for repairs 12/10/31–4/8/34. During 1939–40 participated in bombardment of Finnish coastal positions. Following outbreak of war with Germany retreated to Leningrad and remained there for the duration of hostilities. Was damaged by gunfire of German shore batteries off Kronstadt on 23/9/41 and again when bombed by German aircraft at Leningrad 4/4/42. Paid-off and scrapped in 1956.

Name	Builder	Laid down	Launched	Completed
Sevastopol	Baltisky Zavod (St. Petersburg)	13.7.09	29.6.11	17.11.14

Renamed *Parizhskaya Kommuna* before May 1925 and recommissioned on 17/9/25. Transferred to the Black Sea during 1929–30 incurring heavy weather damage en-route which necessitated a return to Brest for temporary repairs. During 1941–42 was engaged in shelling German positions near Sevastopol and on the Kertch peninsula. Following bomb damage by German aircraft she withdrew to Poti and remained unrepaired and idle for the remainder of the war. Reverted to original name *Sevastopol* in 1943. Repaired post-war and finally scrapped about 1957.

Name	Builder	Laid down	Launched	Completed
Petropavlovsk	Baltisky Zavod (St. Petersburg)	13.7.09	9.9.11	3.11.15

The only battleship in commission after the end of the Civil War. Renamed *Marat* in 1923, under repair 1928–31, and was present at the British Coronation Review in 1937. In 1939 was engaged in shelling Finnish shore positions and received light damage. Was again damaged by gunfire of German shore batteries off Kronstadt during 1941, and was finally bombed and sunk by German aircraft (Stuka Geschw. 2) on 23/9/41 at Kronstadt, when whole of bow—including "A" turret—was destroyed. As she settled on an even keel in very shallow water, with hull and superstructure above water, she was used as a beached floating battery as machinery and both after turrets were operative. Later, "B" turret was also put in working order. Reverted to original name *Petropavlovsk* in 1943, and was scrapped without ever being refloated about 1950.

Name	Builder	Laid down	Launched	Completed
Imperator Aleksander III	Russud-Yard, Nikolaiev	30.10.11	13.4.14	 17

Renamed *Volya* 29/4/17; commissioned without trials 28/6/17, and came under German control in 1918 and British control 1919 before being turned over to White Russian forces when she was again renamed *General Alekseyev* (1919). Interned at Bizerte 1920, taken over by France 1924, and scrapped 1936.

Name	Builder	Laid down	Launched	Completed
Imperatritsa Maria	Russud-Yard	30.10.11	1.11.13	6.7.15

Lost by accidental explosion at Sevastopol 20/10/16, refloated upside down 1917 but again sunk 1920, refloated once more and scrapped in 1927.

Name	Builder	Laid down	Launched	Completed
Yekaterina II	Nikolaiev State Yard	1.9.12	6.6.14	18.10.15

Renamed *Svobodnaya Rossiya* (1917) and scuttled by Red Russian forces at Novorossisk 18/6/18 to prevent her falling into White Russian or German hands.

Of the seven modern battleships commissioned before October 1917 six survived the First World War, but two were lost during the ensuing Civil War while another was irreparably damaged. Consequently, only three—*Gangut*, *Sevastopol*, and *Petropavlovsk*—were taken over by the Soviet Navy in 1922; and all were in need of repair owing to damage received in forcing a passage through ice from Helsinki to Kronstadt in 1918, and during the Kronstadt mutiny of 1921, plus general neglect.

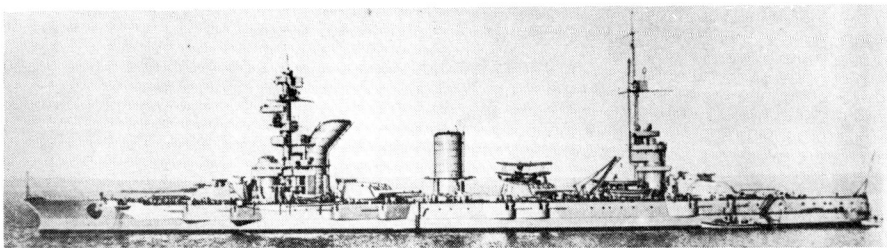

A prewar view of the MARAT. *Note the seaplane stowed on No. 3 turret and aircraft cranes, as well as additional light A.A. guns on the fore and after turrets* [PW/JM

When taken in hand for repair and modernisation between 1928–34 the fore funnel was heightened and angled back to keep the bridge clear of smoke, gunnery control arrangements were improved, and tripod masts and heavy cranes were fitted: the latter for handling seaplanes or light MTBs.

During the 1930s all were re-boilered and *Oktyabrskaya Revolutsia* was probably re-engined with turbine machinery that had been intended for the battlecruiser *Izmail* (never completed). All originally had twenty-five boilers fitted for mixed (coal and oil) firing and they were replaced by oil-fired units, and the designed output of the turbine machinery was 57,500 (ahead)/3,500 (astern) S.H.P.

When refitted at Sevastopol in 1936–39 *Parizhskaya Kommuna* probably received anti-torpedo bulges which increased her beam to about 105 feet (32·00 m.). Shell carried was 1,200 rounds for the 12-inch (305 mm.) guns, 4,000 rounds for the 4·7-inch (120 mm.) guns, 2,100 rounds for the 76 mm. A.A. guns, and a large supply for the 13·2 mm. A.A. machine guns. The 12-inch guns could range up to 25,000 m. except those of *Oktyabrskaya Revolutsia* which had less elevation and were 1,000 m. short compared with those on her sister vessels.

"Poltava" class: **MARAT, OKTYABRSKAYA REVOLUTSIA, PARIZHSKAYA KOMMUNA**

Displacement:	25,464 tons (26,692 tons full load) except *Marat* 25,000 tons (26,170 tons full load).
Dimensions:	590½ (pp) 606½ (oa) × 88¼ (105 over bulges in *Parizhskaya Kommuna*) × 30½/31/31½ (respectively) feet (180·00/184·85 × 26·88/32·00 × 9·30/9·47/9·60 m.).
Machinery:	Twenty-two Yarrow-Admiralty (*Marat*) or twelve Yarrow-Normand (*Oktyabrskaya Revolutsia*) or twenty-five Yarrow (*Parizhskaya Kommuna*) boilers; four shafts; Parsons SR geared turbines S.H.P. 61,000 (*Marat*)/57,500 (*Oktyabrskaya Revolutsia*)/50,000 (*Parizhskaya Kommuna*) = 23 knots.
Bunkers and radius:	O.F. 1,900 except *Marat* 2,050 tons; 1,290 except *Marat* 1,120/2,700 miles @ 23/14 knots.
Protection:	Main belt 8⅞-inch (225 mm.—amid)–4⅞-inch (125 mm.—ends), main deck 1/1½-inch (25/37 mm.), longitudinal bulkheads 1⅞-inch (50 mm.). Turrets 4⅛/8-inch (105/203 mm.)., casemates 5-inch (127 mm.), C.T. 10-inch (254 mm.).
Armament:	Twelve 12-inch (305 mm.—4 × 3), sixteen 4·7-inch (120 mm.—16 × 1), six 3-inch A.A. (76 mm.—6 × 1), thirty-six 13·2 mm. A.A. (6 × 4 & 12 × 1/ . . × . & . . × .) guns; four 17·7-inch (450 mm.—fixed & submerged—sixteen torpedoes) T.T.
Complement:	1,286 (*Marat*)/1,277 (*Oktyabrskaya Revolutsia*)/1,400 (*Parizhskaya Kommuna*).

Shortly before, or during, the Second World War some of the 4·7-inch (120 mm.) guns were removed, together with the cranes and torpedo tubes, so that the anti-aircraft armament could be augmented. At least eight 3·9-inch (100 mm.) and twelve 37 mm. A.A. guns were added in *Oktyabrskaya Revolutsia,* some seven 76 mm. A.A. in *Marat,* and several 76 mm. and six 37 mm. A.A. in *Parizhskaya Kommuna.*

After 1942 the crews of these battleships fought ashore for some time, and the vessels were employed as floating batteries. Their heavy guns played an important part during the Soviet defence of Sevastopol in 1942 and the offensive around Leningrad in 1944.

The MARAT *during a visit to the U.K. for the Coronation Review in 1937. The trunked back forefunnel to keep bridge clear of smoke was a characteristic of all three Soviet-modernised ex-Tsarist battleships* [NMM

Quarter view of the MARAT *in 1937*

[NMM

A wartime view of the OKTYABRSKAYA REVOLUTSIA *with additional A.A. guns on the centre turrets. The aircraft are no longer carried* [S. Breyer coll.

The OKTYABRSKAYA REVOLUTSIA *stripped and ready for scrapping at Kronstadt in October 1956. Note the icebreaking bow* [*USSR*

The SEVASTOPOL *(ex-*PARIZHSKAYA KOMMUNA*). Note the large aircraft boom high on the mainmast*
[*JM BfZ*

During 1934–35, when it was decided that the Soviet Navy was to be expanded so that it could operate outside traditional home waters, the Naval Staff were compelled to advise that the construction of capital ships was beyond the capability of the Soviet heavy industry although 20 years earlier, under a much criticised Czarist regime, this had been possible. (See *Note* 1). Tenders were therefore sought abroad for complete battleships and for machinery, armour plate, and heavy guns for hulls to be built in the Soviet Union.

Among the American firms contacted were the Midwell Steel Co., Bethlehem Steel Co., Gibbs & Cox (naval architects), New York Shipbuilding Corp., Newport News Shipbuilding & Dry Dock Co., and a consortium of firms in the Puget Sound area led by G. C. Nickum & Sons (naval architects). Plans were submitted for the construction of at least one 62,000-ton battleship in the United States, to be armed with nine 16-inch (406 mm.) guns and delivered complete with 900 rounds of A.P. shell. The Soviet Government was prepared to spend $60 to 100m on this project, but as some of the American companies were unwilling to participate in the construction of such a powerful unit for a potentially hostile foreign power, the Soviet Government negotiated with the U.S. Government for the construction of a 45,000-ton battleship in a U.S. Naval Yard. This request was acceded to on 1/6/38, but six months later the Soviet Government withdrew on the grounds that the plans submitted were not suitable. They were, however, prepared to purchase 16-inch guns complete with turrets, fire control equipment, and heavy shell required for battleships building in the Soviet Union. The Soviet Government also contacted the French Schneider-Creusot works for heavy guns, possibly of a larger calibre (17·7-inch/450 mm.), but nothing came of this enquiry.

After nearly three years of negotiations the outbreak of the Second World War brought to a halt all Soviet proposals for building battleships in the United States, and all American shipbuilding capacity was now required for their own needs.

Note 1: Before 1930 the Soviet engineer A. N. Krylov had prepared the design of a 33,000-ton battleship, dimensions $738\frac{1}{4} \times 114\frac{3}{4} \times 29\frac{1}{2}$ feet (225·00 × 35·00 × 9·00 m.), and powered by turbines of 100,000 S.H.P. for a speed of 30 knots, but this design was only preliminary. It is possible that certain features were incorporated in later designs.

The Soviet Navy, however, retained several American designs for capital ships of 35,000 tons, 45,000 tons, and 62,000 tons; and the most interesting was Gibbs & Cox design No. 10581 of 2/3/38. This projected battleship had a full load displacement of 74,000 tons, and in addition to being armed with twelve 16-inch (406 mm.) and twenty 5-inch (127 mm.) guns had a small flight deck amidships above the level of the main battery, with the superstructure arranged off the centreline. The flight deck was only used for landing, and planes were launched from two catapults at the stern. Aircraft were moved from the hangars and flight deck to the stern by a track laid on the port side. Turbines totalling 300,000 S.H.P. drove six shafts for a speed of 34 knots.

During the 1930s there was fairly close collaboration between the Soviet Navy and Italian shipyards despite the marked ideological differences. Italian naval engineers had assisted with the construction of the first Soviet MTBs, submarines, destroyers, and cruisers; Italian diesel engines were installed in Soviet submarines; and orders were placed in Italian yards for two large patrol vessels for the Pacific and a fast flotilla leader for the Black Sea. However, this did not deter Italian submarines from sinking Soviet merchant ships bringing aid to Republican forces in Spain during the Civil War.

Nevertheless Soviet enquiries for battleships were also extended to Italy, and on 16/7/36 Ansaldo proposed a vessel (known as Project U.P.41) of 42,000 tons standard displacement (45,470 tons normal load), with dimensions of $816\frac{3}{4} \times 116\frac{1}{2} \times 30\frac{3}{4}$ feet (249·00 × 35·50 × 9·40 m.), and to be powered by turbines of 177,538 S.H.P. for a speed of 32 knots. The armament was to comprise nine 16-inch (406 mm.— 3 × 3), twelve 7·1-inch (180 mm.—4 × 3), twenty-four 3·9-inch A.A. (100 mm.—12 × 2), forty-eight 45 mm. A.A. (12 × 4), and twenty-four 13·2 mm. A.A. (12 × 2) guns; and four aircraft with one catapult. Protection both above and below water was very strong, and was even superior to that for the "Vittorio Veneto" class (designed at about the same time) to which the project bore a marked resemblance. The heavy anti-aircraft armament was a remarkable feature for the time.

Finally, as a result of the German-Soviet treaty of 1939, Germany was asked to submit plans of a 50,000-ton battleship of the "Bismarck" class. The German Naval Staff demurred but some of this information was made available by 1940. Orders were also placed for 16-inch (406 mm.), 15-inch (381 mm),

11-inch (280 mm.) and 6·1-inch (155 mm) guns in turrets; torpedoes and launch tubes; and other naval equipment. The manufacture of sixteen 15-inch guns and eight twin turrets was undertaken in Germany, and by August 1941 eight guns and one turret were completed but none were ever delivered to the Soviet Navy owing to the outbreak of hostilities between the two countries. Some material for the construction of battleships or battlecruisers was also ordered from various other European firms, e.g. engine parts from the Swiss Brown-Boven & Co., Baden, but never delivered for the same reason.

Two large battleships were eventually laid down in Soviet yards during 1938, and their design was undoubtedly influenced by the numerous Soviet enquiries put out abroad. According to German Naval Intelligence sources—based on captured documents, interrogation, and aerial photographs—these vessels had the following main particulars:

Project 23: **SOVIETSKY SOYUZ, SOVIETSKAYA UKRAINA**

Displacement: 59,000 tons (59,000 tons normal load, 65,000 tons full load).

Dimensions: 859½ × 131¼ × 32¾ feet (262·00 × 40·00 × 10·00 m.) or 876 (oa) × 139 (probably across bulges) × . . . . (267·00 × 42·37 × . . . . m.).

Machinery: Four shafts, geared turbines for 32 knots.

Armament: Nine 16-inch (406 mm.—3 × 3), twelve 6-inch (152 mm.—6 × 2), twenty-four 3·9-inch A.A. (12 × 2), forty-eight 37 mm. A.A. (24 × 2), twenty-four 12·7 mm. A.A. (12 × 2) guns; four aircraft and one catapult.

The design was undoubtedly influenced by the Ansaldo project, and was modified several times during the course of construction. Difficulty was also experienced in the manufacture of 16-inch (406 mm.) guns, and only one experimental piece of this calibre had been produced prior to the German invasion in 1941. This gun was subsequently incorporated in a coastal battery at Leningrad. Although two/three turrets had been produced, the inability to provide guns—even from foreign sources—made the construction of these battleships senseless. For these reasons, and because war experience had shown that capital ships could not be operated without air cover, the construction of these vessels was first slowed down and finally brought to a halt. There was also a shortage in the supply of steel, and Soviet industry could not provide for both battleships and the large tank programmes that had been put in hand.

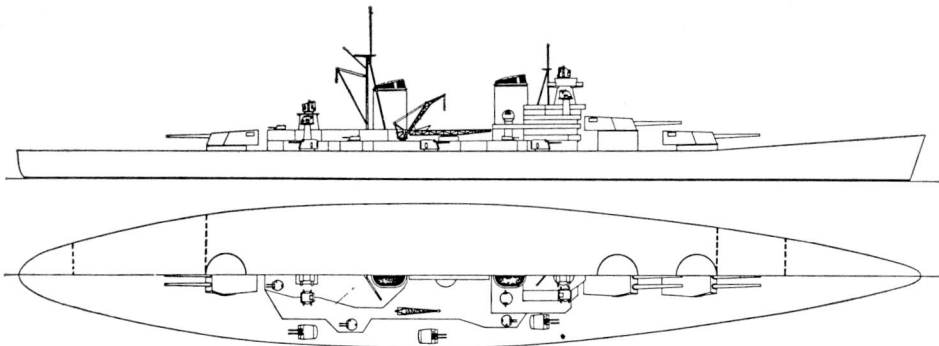

The projected plan of "Sovietsky Soyuz" class battleships, prepared from all available information [S. Breyer

(Above) A German aerial photograph of the SOVIETSKAYA UKRAINA *under construction at Nikolaiev in 1941. Note the barbettes for main turrets* [JM/BfZ

(Right) A closer view of the SOVIETSKAYA UKRAINA, *showing a barbette in the foreground and marked sheer to the hull forward* [JM/BfZ

Name	Builder	Laid down	Remains
Sovietsky Soyuz	Ordzhonikidze Yard (Leningrad)	28.8.38	Hull scrapped on slip post-war.
Sovietskaya Ukraina	Marti South Yard (Nikolaiev)	....11.38	Incomplete and damaged hull scrapped on slip post-war.

One unit had been laid down at the Ordzhonikidze Yard (Leningrad) on 28/8/38 but construction was practically stopped by late 1940. The hull structure was essentially complete and ready for launching by mid-1941 with the machinery and deck armour in place. However, most of the armour was removed between 1941–44, and after the war the hull was cut into sections on the slip and scrapped. It is possible that the names proposed for this vessel was first *Lenin*, and later *Sovietsky Soyuz*.

The other unit was laid down at the Marti South Yard (Nikolaiev) in 11/38 but construction was slowed down in late 1940. When the German Army occupied Nikolaiev on 16/8/41 the vessel was 66% complete and launching was scheduled for 11/42. When the Germans evacuated Nikolaiev in 1944 they destroyed the slip under the hull, giving it a list of 5/10 deg. to port, and so effectively prevented its completion by the Soviet Navy and there was no alternative except to scrap the hull. It is possible that the names proposed for this vessel were first *Stalin*, and later *Sovietskaya Ukraina*.

Had these vessels been completed they would have only been surpassed by the Japanese "Yamato" class in size and armament, but they were beyond the capability of Soviet industry.

Following the Italian surrender in 1943 the Soviet Government claimed one-third of Italian Fleet now under Allied control. As it was not possible to settle, far less implement, this claim while the war was still in progress the American and British navies transferred certain of their own units to the Soviet Navy to be returned when the allocation of Italian tonnage had been accomplished.

The Royal Navy transferred the battleship *Royal Sovereign* and four submarines, and the United States Navy the cruiser *Milwaukee* and nine old destroyers of the "flush-decked" type which were on loan to the Royal Navy under Lend/Lease.

A Soviet crew arrived in the U.K. early in 1944 and commissioned the *Arkhangelsk* (ex-*Royal Sovereign*) on 30/5/44 and she left with convoy JW.59 for the Kola Inlet on 24/8/44. The *Arkhangelsk* remained completely inactive in the Arctic for the remainder of the war, and was returned to the Royal Navy on 4/2/49. She arrived at Inverkeithing 18/5/49 for scrapping by T. W. Ward.

Ex-British "Royal Sovereign" class: **ARKHANGELSK**

Displacement:	29,150 tons (32,500 tons full load).
Dimensions:	580 (pp) 620½ (oa) × 88½ (101½ over bulges) × 28½ (32 full load) feet (176·77/190·95 × 26·98/30·94 × 8·69/9·76 m.).
Machinery:	Eighteen Babcock & Wilcox boilers; four shafts; Parsons turbines S.H.P. 40,000 = 23 (21½ full load) knots.
Bunkers and radius	O.F. 3,230 tons; . . . ./4,200 miles @ . ./. . knots.
Protection:	Main belt 13-inch (330 mm.—amid)–4/6-inch (102/152 mm.—ends), upper belt 6-inch (152 mm.), bulkheads closing belts 4/6-inch (102/152 mm.), longitudinal bulkheads 1/1½-inch (25/37 mm.). Fo'c'sle deck ¾/1-inch (20/25 mm.—amid), upper deck 1¼/1½-inch (32/37 mm.—amid), main deck 1 (flat)/2(slope) (25/51 mm.—amid), lower deck 1/2½-inch (25/64 mm.—fwd.)–2½-inch (64 mm.—aft) with 3/4-inch (76/102 mm.) over steering gear. Turrets 13-inch (330 mm.—face)–11-inch (280 mm.—sides and rear)–5-inch (127 mm.—overhang)–4¾-inch (108 mm.—crown), barbettes 7/10-inch (178/254 mm.)–4/6-inch (102/152 mm.), casemates 6-inch (152 mm). Fwd. C. T. 11-inch (280 mm.) and aft C.T. 6-inch (152 mm).
Armament:	Eight 15-inch (381 mm.—4 × 2), twelve 6-inch (152 mm.—12 × 1), eight 4-inch A.A. (102 mm.—4 × 2), thirty-two 2-pounder A.A. (40 mm.—4 × 8), seventeen 20 mm. A.A. (17 × 1) guns.
Complement:	1,146.

In 1944 the Royal Navy were laying up in reserve the "Royal Sovereign" class battleships as they were surplus to operational requirements. Consequently there was no objection to one being transferred to the Soviet Navy. The photograph shows the ARKHANGELSK *(ex-*ROYAL SOVEREIGN*) with standard war modifications* [IWM

Name	Builder	Launched	Fate
Arkhangelsk (ex-R.N. *Royal Sovereign*)	H.M. Dockyard (Portsmouth)	29.4.15	Returned R.N. 4/2/49; sold T. W. Ward and arrived Inverkeithing 18/5/49 for scrapping.

BATTLECRUISERS

What has been referred to as the "little" Naval Programme of 1912 made financial provision for the construction of four battlecruisers, eight light cruisers, thirty-six destroyers, and eighteen submarines; of which two cruisers and six submarines were earmarked for the Far East, and two cruisers for the Black Sea.

The four battlecruisers were of 32,500 tons, armed with twelve 14-inch (356 mm.—4 × 3) and twenty-four 5·1-inch (130 mm.) guns, and had a projected speed of 29½ knots. They were all laid down before the outbreak of the First World War, and their fates were as follows:

Name	Builder	Launched	Fate
Borodino	New Admiralty Yard (St. Petersburg)	1.7.15	Never completed, scrapped Bremen 1923.
Izmail	—do—	22.6.15	Never completed, scrapped Leningrad 1931.
Navarin	—do—	22.11.16	Never completed, scrapped Hamburg 1923.
Kinburn	—do—	30.10.15	Never completed, scrapped Kiel 1923.

None of these vessels were completed by 1917, and as there was little likelihood of all their machinery being delivered by British sub-contractors, their construction was cancelled as Soviet industry could not undertake the manufacture of steam turbines.

Among the heavy surface ships proposed for an ocean-going Soviet Navy in 1934–35 were smaller editions of the battleships which were logically referred to as battlecruisers, owing to their high speed, although there is no clear indication that they were considered as such by the Soviet Navy. It may have been intended to arm them with the 14-inch guns ordered for the "Borodino" class, but as a result of the German-Soviet pact of 1939 their main armament of 15-inch guns and twin turrets were ordered in Germany but were finally never supplied.

Battlecruisers: **STRANA SOVIETOV, SOVIETSKAYA BIELOROSSIYA**

Displacement:	35,000 tons.
Dimensions:	770 × 110 × .. feet (234·70 × 33·55 × .... m.).
Machinery:	Four shafts, geared turbines S.H.P. 150,000 = 32 knots.
Armament:	Eight 15-inch (381 mm.—4 × 2), and numerous 3·9-inch A.A. (100 mm.), 37 mm. A.A. and 12·7 mm. A.A. guns.

First ship was laid down on 15/7/39 at the Marti Yard (Leningrad), and construction was suspended in late 1940. Much material was removed during the war, and after the war the hull was cut up on the slip and expended in weapon experiments in about 1950. Suggested name was *Strana Sovietov.*

The second unit was laid down at the Marti North Yard (Nikolaiev) at the end of 1939, and work was arrested in early 1940 and suspended later in the year. Following the German occupation of Nikolaiev in August 1941 the incomplete hull was scrapped on the slip. Suggested name was *Sovietskaya Bielorossiya.* The appearance of these vessels was to be generally similar to the Italian "Zara" class heavy cruisers.

Several aerial photographs taken of the ship building at Leningrad show the hull without bow and stern sections and led to the erroneous conclusion that it was an aircraft carrier.

AIRCRAFT CARRIERS

As long as the Soviet Navy envisaged its main role as the defence of the inner part of the Gulf of Finland and the coasts of the Black Sea, as it was the case between 1920–32, aircraft carriers were not required. Soviet strategy was based upon the use of mines, destroyers, submarines, and MTBs supported by land-based aircraft, coastal artillery, and the guns of the old battleships.

Note 2: What the Soviet Navy failed to realise was the extent to which the German Navy itself was dependent on foreign help in designing aircraft carriers, with which they had no experience. Japan provided Germany with some assistance but revealed none of their most recent experience in carrier construction.

However, following the creation of the Far East Fleet in 1932, and the Arctic Fleet in the following year, the Soviet Navy regained access to the open oceans and this led to the revision of the coast defence strategy into a wider, oceanic doctrine. As a consequence modern battleships, cruisers, destroyers, and submarines were laid down; and while they could have operated under the cover of shore-based aircraft in the narrow waters of the Baltic and Black Sea, this would not have been possible in the Arctic—far less in the Far East—if any large scale operations were to be mounted.

The Soviet Navy soon appreciated that to build battleships and deny them air cover in an ocean environment was a foolhardy proposition, and they well realised that they lacked the experience to build aircraft carriers. Therefore help was once more sought from abroad, and Germany were asked— as a result of the German-Soviet pact—to supply plans of the *Graf Zeppelin* (see *Note* 2). This request met with a blank refusal: Germany would neither provide the plans or sell a carrier. This, in turn, effected the future use of the two battleships and two battlecruisers under construction, and could well prompted the decision made in late 1940 to slow down, or suspend, all work on them.

The Third 5-year plan for 1938–42 included the construction of two aircraft carriers—probably one large and one small unit—but these were cancelled on Stalin's orders in 1939–40. Therefore such vessels as the *Voroshilov*, *Lyetl*, and others mentioned in several naval reference books never existed.

After the German surrender the Soviet Navy seized the aircraft carrier *Graf Zeppelin* lying about 90% complete at Stettin and only slightly damaged. While en-route from Kaliningrad to Leningrad, in tow, the railroad cars loaded as part of the war reparations on flight and hangar decks shifted in a storm, and the carrier capsized and floundered. Neither the *Graf Zeppelin*, or any other German major units found damaged in ports—the battlecruiser *Gneisenau* at Gydnia, the armoured ship *Lützow* (ex-*Deutschland*) at Swinemünde, or the heavy cruiser *Seydlitz* at Königsberg—were repaired.

SEAPLANE CARRIERS

Between the end of the Civil War and the outbreak of the Second World War the Soviet Navy drew up several plans to convert old warships into seaplane carriers. One unconfirmed report mentioned the old armoured cruiser *Ryurik* (built in the U.K. in 1907), but this failed to materialise owing to the damaged state of the hull and machinery. During the 1930s the old cruiser *Komintern* was taken in hand in the Black Sea for conversion to a seaplane carrier, when her after funnel and some boilers were removed, but work was abandoned soon after as the vessel was too old and slow for this duty.

Shortly before the Second World War two seaplane carriers were projected for the Far East (Pacific) Fleet. They were to be large vessels, generally resembling the Japanese "Midumo" class, fitted with two catapults abaft a single, thin funnel. They were probably planned to operate flying boats from secluded anchorages on the Siberian coast between Vladivostok and the Behring Strait, and were to be built at the Komsomolsk Yard (River Amur) but were most likely cancelled before laying down. None were certainly in service at the close of the war.

CRUISERS

During the Russo-Japanese War 1904–05 the Imperial Russian Navy lost five armoured and six protected cruisers, while two armoured and nine protected cruisers survived the conflict. Between 1906–14 only the British-built large armoured cruiser *Ryurik* and three smaller Russian-built armoured cruisers were added to the Baltic Fleet. Ten protected cruisers were building, or on order, at the outbreak of the First World War.

Of this total, two 4,500-ton cruisers to be armed with eight 5-inch (127 mm.—8 × 1) guns were building in Germany and were requisitioned for the German Navy, with the remainder equally divided between Baltic and Black Sea yards. The former were vessels of 6,800/7,600 tons to be armed with twelve 6-inch (152 mm.) guns, while the latter were also vessels of 7,600 tons to be armed with fifteen 5-inch (127 mm.) guns.

In the course of the First World War the Imperial Navy salved a Turkish light cruiser which had been mined; purchased a Japanese cruiser (a former Imperial Navy ship which had been sunk during the 1904–05 war but had been salved); and lost one armoured and one protected cruiser as a result of enemy action. In 1918 the former Turkish light cruiser was retroceded.

In the Civil War period 1918–22 one protected cruiser was sunk by British CMBs off Kronstadt, and a second accompanied the White Russian fleet to internment in Bizerte and was ultimately scrapped by the French. All other cruisers left in Soviet Navy hands were so worn out or damaged that they had to be paid-off with the exception of two old cruisers of no combatant value, the *Avrora* in the Baltic and the *Pamyat Merkurya* in the Black Sea.

None of the eight light cruisers under construction were completed during the First World War, or the ensuing Civil War, and the Soviet Navy were ultimately only able to continue the construction of three of them. The fates of the cruisers which survived the Civil War in Soviet hands was as follows:

Rossiya: lost in tow while en-route to breakers Baltic 1922,

Gromoboi: scrapped Bremen 1922,

Diana: scrapped Bremen 1922,

Varyag: lost in tow while en-route to breakers in U.K. early 1920 and wreck broken up by German salvage firms 1923-25,

Avrova: recommissioned Baltic as a training vessel.

Askold: interned in U.K. 1920 and scrapped Hamburg 1922,

Bogatyr: scrapped Bremen 1922,

Pamyat Merkurya: recommissioned Black Sea, as training vessel renamed *Komintern.*

Admiral Makarov: scrapped Stettin 1922.

Bayan: scrapped Stettin 1922,

Ryurik: never repaired after being mined and stranding during war, retained as hulk until 1930s when scrapped.

The fates of the ten cruisers building for the Imperial Navy at the outbreak of the First World War was as follows:

Name	Builder	Laid down	Launched	Completed
Admiral Nevelskoy	Schichau (Danzig)	....2.13	21.11.14	1.9.15

Requisitioned and German Navy *Elbing* (1914), lost in collision with German battleship *Posen* at Battle of Jutland 1/6/16.

Murayev Amursky	Schichau (Danzig)	....2.13	11.4.14	14.12.14

Requisitioned and German Navy *Pillau* (1914), allocated to Italy under terms of Peace Treaty and renamed *Bari* (1920), bombed by American aircraft Livorno ../9/43 and subsequently scrapped.

Admiral Boutakov	Putilov (St. Petersburg)	25.11.13	5.8.16	—

Construction abandoned but hull survived until after Second World War when it was expended as a breakwater at the mouth of the River Neva. Scrapped 1952.

Admiral Spiridov	Putilov (St. Petersburg)	29.11.13	9.9.16	—

Completed as mercantile tanker *Groznyeft* (1926), renamed *Grozny* (1935), captured by Germans 8/10/41 and scuttled at Mariupol 20/9/43.

Admiral Greig	...... (Reval)	7.11.13	9.12.16	—

Construction suspended 1917–22 and completed as mercantile tanker *Aznyeft* (1926). Broke apart and sank in a storm off Batum, Black Sea, in the 1930s.

| Svetlana | Russian Shipbuilding (Reval) | 7.12.13 | 27.11.15 | ....28 |

Towed to St. Petersburg 1916, construction suspended 1917–22. Renamed *Klara Zetkin* while under construction (1924), then *Sovnarkom*, and *Profintern* (1927). Completed to a modified design and commissioned in 1928; transferred to Black Sea 1929, and again renamed *Krasny Krim* (1939). Decommissioned 1958, scrapped 1960.

| Admiral Istomin | Nikolaiev (Black Sea) | .... 15 | — | — |

Construction abandoned and scrapped on slip when 40% complete after the Civil War.

| Admiral Kornilov | Nikolaiev (Black Sea) | .... 15 | — | — |

Construction abandoned and scrapped on slip when 45% complete after the Civil War.

| Admiral Nakhimov | Nikolaiev (Black Sea) | 31.10.13 | 6.11.15 | 27.2.27 |

Construction suspended 1917–22, renamed *Chervonaya Ukraina* on 31/12/22 while under construction, and completed to a modified design. Commissioned 1927. Bombed German aircraft at Sevastopol 12/11/41, and foundered following day.

| Admiral Lazarev | Nikolaiev (Black Sea) | 31.10.13 | 21.6.16 | 25.1.32 |

Construction suspended 1917–24 when renamed *Krasny Kavkaz*. Work resumed same year, and ship completed to a different design. Commissioned 25/1/32. Expended as target 6/50.

Vulcan type: **KOMINTERN** (B)

The machinery of this vessel was destroyed during the British occupation of Sevastopol during 1919, and she was consequently left behind when the White Russian forces finally evacuated South Russia in 1920. She was subsequently repaired by the Soviet Navy and renamed *Komintern* when placed in commission 1/5/23. Used as a training ship, her speed was well below 20 knots, and during the 1930s it was proposed to convert the *Komintern* into a seaplane carrier on lines similar to the Swedish *Gotland*. Her armament was probably reduced before 1939, when the submerged T.T. were also removed, and the A.A. armament augmented during the war.

During the Second World War this vessel took part in the defence and evacuation of Odessa in 1941, and the defence of Sevastopol in 1942. She was heavily damaged when bombed by German aircraft at Novorossisk on 2/7/42. On reaching Poti, she was again bombed on 16/7/42 and was written-off as a constructive total loss, and was expended soon after as an additional breakwater at Poti.

Displacement:	6,338 tons.
Dimensions:	440¼ (pp) .... (oa) × 54½ × 22¼ feet (134·20/...... × 16·60 × 6·80 m.).
Machinery:	Sixteen Normand boilers; two shafts; Reciprocating (VTE) I.H.P. 19,500 = 23 knots.
Bunkers and radius:	Coal 1,100 tons; 5,300 miles @ 12 knots.
Protection:	Main deck 1½-inch (35 mm.)–2¾-inch (70 mm.), casemates 3-inch (76 mm.), C.T. 5½-inch (140 mm.).
Armament:	Ten 5·1-inch (130 mm.—10 × 1), six 75 mm. (6 × 1), three 3-inch A.A. (76 mm.—3 × 1), two 47 mm. (2 × 1), and two machine (2 × 1) guns.
Complement:	590.

Name	Builder	Laid down	Launched	Completed
Komintern (ex-*Pamyat Merkurya*, ex-*Kagoul*)	State Yard (Nikolaiev)	00	4.10.02	05

The training cruiser KOMINTERN *before reconstruction*

[USSR

Admiralty type: **AVRORA (B)**

This vessel was present at Tsushima and was able to escape, in a damaged condition, to Manila where she was interned for the remainder of the Russo-Japanese War. She later returned to the Baltic, and after a passive role during the First World War was credited with firing the first shot of the October Revolution.

After the Civil War the *Avrora* was used as a training ship and was permanently stationed at Leningrad after 1930. During 1941 she was briefly engaged in bombarding German positions near Oranienbaum before she sank in shallow water near Lomonossov after being bombed by German aircraft. Her guns were removed and were used ashore by the armoured train *Baltiyets*. Following the close of the war the *Avrora* was salved and converted into a floating museum.

Displacement:	5,622 tons.
Dimensions:	416¾ (pp) .... × 55¼ × 21 feet (127·00/.... × 16·80 × 6·40 m.).
Machinery:	Twenty-four Belleville boilers; three shafts; reciprocating (HTE) I.H.P. 12,000 = 18 knots.
Bunkers and *radius:*	Coal 960 tons; 2,000 miles @ 11 knots.
Protection:	Main deck 1¾–2¾-inch (50/70 mm.), casemates and shields 3-inch (76 mm.), C.T. 6-inch (152 mm.).
Armament:	Ten 5·1-inch (130 mm.—10 × 1), four 75 mm. (4 × 1), two 3-inch A.A. (76 mm.— 2 × 1), four machine (4 × 1) guns; two 17·7-inch (450 mm.—fixed and submerged) T.T.
Complement:	598.

Name	Builder	Laid down	Launched	Completed
Avrora (ex-*SSSR*, ex-*Avrora*)	Galerny Yard (St. Petersburg)	96	24.5.00	02

The AVRORA *preserved as a naval relic*

[*USSR*

Admiralty type: **CHERVONAYA UKRAINA** (BS)

This vessel was under construction for nearly 15 years and her design was quite outdated when finally completed. Ten of the guns were carried low at main deck level (six arranged in casemates) and were difficult to work in adverse weather. The machinery was well behind contemporary practice, and not surprisingly the designed speed—32 knots—was not attained, while the best possible speed was under 25 knots in 1941. One seaplane (handled by a crane) had been carried prior to the Second World War but had been removed, and during the war the torpedo armament was probably reduced so as the A.A. armament could be augmented. The 3-inch (76 mm.) A.A. were replaced by twelve 37 mm. A.A. guns. After being bombed and sunk in shallow water by German aircraft at Sevastopol some guns were removed for use ashore before the wrecked vessel was again hit by bombs on 2/4/42 and completely destroyed.

Displacement:	6,934 tons.
Dimensions:	519¾ (pp) .... (oa) × 49¼ × 21¼ feet (158·40/...... × 15·30 × 6·50 m.).
Machinery:	Thirteen Yarrow boilers; two shafts; Parsons turbines S.H.P. 50,000 = 29½ knots.
Bunkers and radius:	O.F. 690 tons and coal 540 tons; 3,700 miles @ 18 knots.
Protection:	Main deck 1-inch (25 mm.), casemates and gun shields 1¾-inch (50 mm.), C.T. 3-inch (76 mm.).
Armament:	Fifteen 5·1-inch (130 mm.—15 × 1), four 3-inch A.A. (76 mm.—4 × 1), twelve machine (.. × ..) guns; twelve 21-inch (533 mm.—4 × 3) T.T.; one hundred mines.
Complement:	684/750.

A prewar view of the CHERVONAYA UKRAINA. *Note the seaplane stowed between the 2nd and 3rd funnels*
[JM

Admiralty type: **KRASNY KRIM** (BS).

Original design was modified to increase bow fire, and as completed—after being under construction for over ten years—this vessel generally resembled *Chervonaya Ukraina*. The same remarks apply as to positioning of guns and machinery. As this vessel was first stationed in the Baltic side armour was not fitted so as the hull could be strengthened for navigation in ice, but she was later transferred to the Black Sea in 1929–30 in company with the battleship *Parizhskaya Kommuna*.

During the war two banks of T.T. were removed and the A.A. armament augmented by the probable addition of two 3·9-inch (100 mm.) and ten 37 mm. guns. A seaplane (handled by a crane) had been carried pre-war but was removed. During the war she was employed in bombarding German-held positions in the Crimea in 1941–42 and acted as a fast troop transport during the siege of Sevastopol. Although it has been frequently stated that the *Krasny Krim* was torpedoed by an Italian MTB off the Crimea in 1942 this, in fact, did not occur.

Displacement: 6,934 tons.

Dimensions: 487 (pp) .... (oa) × 50½ × 18½ feet (154·50/.... × 15·40 × 5·60 m.).

Machinery: Thirteen Yarrow boilers, two shafts; Brown-Curtis turbines S.H.P. 50,000 = 29 knots.

Bunkers and
radius: O.F. 2,900 tons; 3,700 miles @ 18 knots.

Protection: Main deck 1-inch (25 mm.), casemates and gun shields 2-inch (50 mm.), C.T. 3-inch (76 mm.).

Armament: Fifteen 5·1-inch (130 mm.—15 × 1), four 3·9-inch A.A. (100 mm.—4 × 1), four 45 mm. A.A. (4× 1) guns; twelve 21-inch (533 mm.—4 × 3) T.T.; one hundred mines.

Complement: 684.

(Right) The CHERVONAYA UKRAINA *in mid-1930s (top) and* KRASNY KRIM *in 1940 (lower)* [S. Breyer

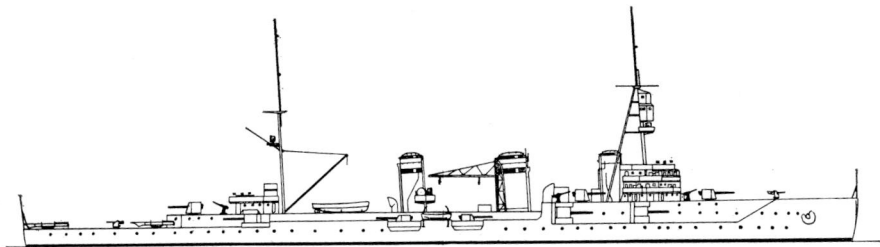

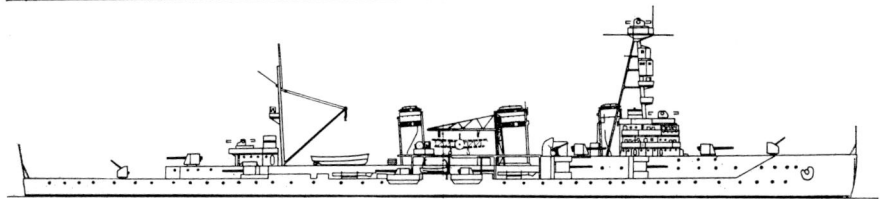

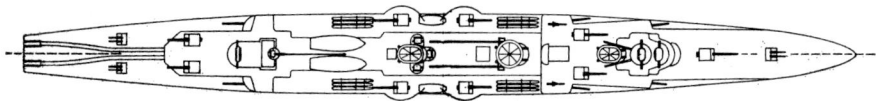

A prewar view of the CHERVONAYA UKRAINA *for comparison with* KRASNY KRIM *(right)* [*USSR*

58

The old broadside cruiser KRASNY KRIM *showing additional A.A. guns on the fo'c'sle and seaplane between the 2nd and 3rd funnels. Note large rangefinder on the bridge* [JM

Admiralty type: **KRASNY KAVKAZ** (BS)

Originally a sister vessel to the *Chervonaya Ukraina* the design was considerably modified to ship a heavier calibre armament mounted in turrets on the centre line and as such superior to the original broadside arrangement. These alterations delayed her completion—even by Soviet standards—so that she was under construction for nearly 20 years. Shortly after completion the *Krasny Kavkaz* was heavily damaged following collision with the cruiser *Komintern*, and she was lengthened by some 14/15 feet (4–4·5 in.) when a new stem was fitted.

Two aircraft and a catapult were originally carried but these, together with two banks of T.T., were removed before (or shortly after) the outbreak of the Second World War so that the A.A. armament could be augmented. During the war the single 3·9-inch A.A. (100 mm.) guns were replaced by twin mountings. Damaged by the gunfire of German coastal batteries off Feodosia at the end of 1941, followed by bomb damage to the stern a few days later, the *Krasny Kavkaz* had to be towed away for repair, but was operational again from October 1942 to January 1943, when she was again damaged.

Displacement:	8,030 tons.
Dimensions:	528¼ (pp) 544½ (oa) × 50¼ × 20¼ feet (161·00/166·00 × 15·30 × 6·20 m.).
Machinery:	Ten Yarrow boilers; two shafts; .... turbines S.H.P. 55,000 = 29 knots.
Bunkers and radius:	O.F. 1,600 tons; 7,300 miles @ .. knots.
Protection:	Main deck 1–1½-inch (25/37 mm.), turrets 3-inch (76 mm.), C.T. 3-inch (76 mm.).
Armament:	Four 7·1-inch (180 mm.—4 × 1), six 3·9-inch A.A. (100 mm.—6 × 1), two 3-inch A.A. (76 mm.—2 × 1), four 45 mm. A.A. (4 × 1), eight 37 mm. A.A. (.. × ..) guns; six 21-inch (533 mm—2 × 3) T.T.; one hundred mines.
Complement:	850.

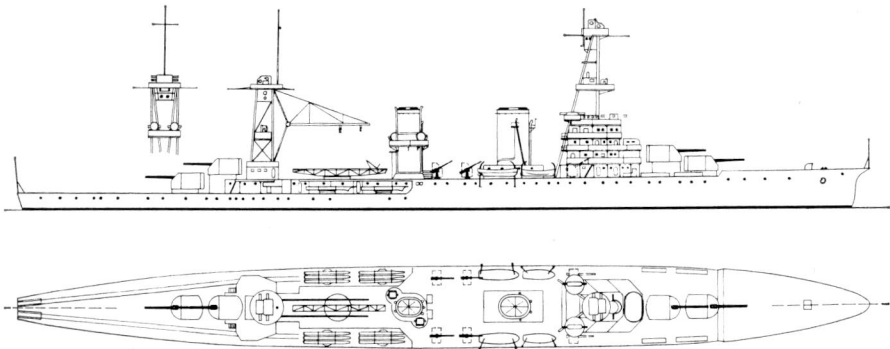

The KRASNY KAVKAZ *in 1940. The catapult and two banks of T.T. were later removed to make space for additional A.A. guns and more boats* [S. Breyer

The KRASNY KAVKAZ *in 1935. Note lattice mainmast and seaplane on the catapult*   JM

Ex-American "Omaha" class: **MURMANSK** (A)

This vessel was transferred to the Soviet Navy—together with a battleship, nine destroyers, and four submarines—as a token contribution until the division of surrendered Italian tonnage could be settled post-war. She accompanied convoy JW-58 and arrived at the Kola inlet on 5/4/44, and was turned over to the Soviet Navy on 20/4/44 when she was renamed *Murmansk*. She spent the remainder of the war in the Arctic and was never involved in action. She was returned to the United States Navy on 8/3/49 and was scrapped at Wilmington later in the year. Originally two aircraft and two catapults were carried, but they were removed prior to transfer.

Displacement:	7,050 tons (9,150 tons full load).
Dimensions:	550 (wl) 555½ (oa) × 55¼ × 14¼ (20 full load) feet (167·64/169·31 × 16·87 × 4.34 6·10 m).
Machinery:	Twelve Yarrow boilers; four shafts; Westinghouse geared turbines S.H.P. 90,000 = 33¾ knots.
Bunkers and radius:	O.F. 2,068 tons; 10,000/3,000 miles @ 15/30 knots.
Protection:	Main belt 3-inch (76 mm.), bulkheads 2–3-inch (51/76 mm.), upper deck 1½-inch (amid—38 mm.), lower deck 1½-inch (ends—38 mm.), casemates and turrets 1–2-inch (25/51 mm).
Armament:	Twelve 6-inch (152 mm.—8 × 1), eight 3-inch (76 mm.—8 × 1) A.A., eight 40 mm. A.A. (2 × 4), fourteen 20 mm. A.A. (14 × 1) guns; six 21-inch (533 mm.—2 × 3) T.T.
Complement:	458.

Name	Builder	Laid down	Launched	Commissioned
Murmansk (ex-U.S.N. *Milwaukee*)	Seattle Construction and Dry Dock	13.12.18	24.3.21	20.6.23 (U.S. Navy) 20.4.44 (Sov. Navy)

War modifications to the MURMANSK *(ex-*U.S.N. MILWAUKEE*) included air warning radar and 40 mm. and 20 mm. A.A. guns* [*JM*

"Kirov" class: First group (*Project* 26) **KIROV** (B), **VOROSHILOV** (BS). *Second group* (*Project* 26b)
MAKSIM GORKI (B), **MOLOTOV** (BS), **KALININ** (P), and **KAGANOVICH** (P)

After the completion of the *Krasny Kavkaz* a new class of cruiser was authorised to mount the new
7·1-inch guns (180 mm.) which had been experimentally mounted in the former vessel. With Italian
technical assistance the first pair were laid down in 1935, followed by another pair the following year,
and a final pair in 1939 for the Pacific Fleet. There were differences in the superstructure and with
rigging between the two groups. A maximum speed of 35·94 knots was attained on trials. They were
originally fitted to carry two aircraft and a catapult, but this was removed after 1941 and the A.A.
armament was augmented during the war.

Displacement:	8,800 tons (11,500 tons full load).
Dimensions :	626$\frac{3}{4}$ (pp) .... (oa) × 59 × 20 feet (191·00/.... × 18·00 × 6·10 m.).
Machinery:	Six Yarrow-Normand boilers; two shafts; ...... geared turbines S.H.P. 113,000 = 35 knots.
Bunkers and radius:	O.F. 1,280 tons; 850/3,000 miles @ 34/18 knots.
Protection:	Main belt 3-inch (75 mm.), main deck 2-inch (50 mm), turrets 4-inch (100 mm.), C.T. 3-inch (75 mm.).
Armament:	Nine 7·1-inch (180 mm.—3 × 3), six 3·9-inch A.A. (100 mm.—6 × 1), six 45 mm. A.A (.. × ..) guns; six 21-inch (533 mm.—2 × 3) T.T.; two aircraft and one catapult; ninety mines and sixty DCs.
Complement:	734.

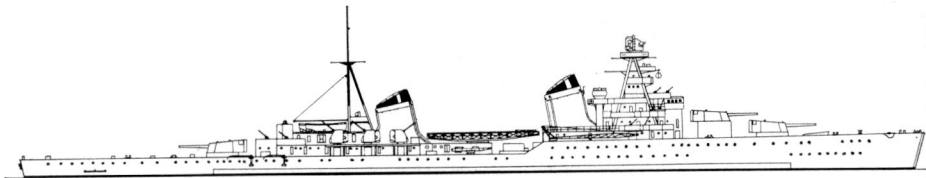

The KIROV *in 1940 (top) and shortly after the war (below)*

[S. Breyer

The KIROV *in 1940. The design of this class of heavy cruisers showed a marked Italian influence*   [JM/BfZ

In the MAKSIM GORKI *the bridgework was modified* [USSR

A wartime view of the VOROSHILOV

[*JM*/*BfZ*

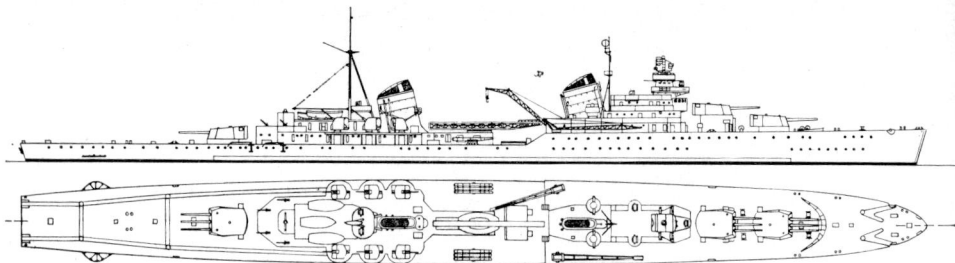

The MAKSIM GORKI *in 1940*

[S. Breyer]

Name	Builder	Laid down	Launched	Completed
Kirov	Ordzhonikidze Yard (Leningrad)	..10.35	1.12.36	12.12.39

Engaged bombarding Finnish shore positions 1939. Bombed and damaged by German aircraft late 1941 and again in early 1942. Repaired and back in service early 1943. Now serving as a headquarters and training ship.

Name	Builder	Laid down	Launched	Completed
Maksim Gorki	Ordzhonikidze Yard (Leningrad)	..10.36	..12.37	12.12.40

Mined and lost bow on 23/6/41 and towed to Leningrad for repair where further damaged by gunfire of German shore battery later in the year, and again hit by seven bombs in early 1942. Repaired and back in service mid-1942. Paid-off late 1950s.

Name	Builder	Laid down	Launched	Completed
Molotov	Marti South Yard (Nikolaiev)	..11.36	23.2.39	14.6.41

Torpedoed by Italian MTB off Crimean coast 3/8/42, returned to Caucasian port where damaged stern was replaced by a section from the incomplete cruiser *Frunze*, and back in service late 1944. Renamed *Slava* (1958).

Name	Builder	Laid down	Launched	Completed
Voroshilov	Marti South Yard (Nikolaiev)	15.10.35	39	15.6.40

Damaged by close mine explosions off Fidonissi Island 1/11/41, repaired, again damaged when hit by three bombs from German aircraft and towed back to Poti for repairs. Scrapped in the 1960s.

Name	Builder	Laid down	Launched	Completed
Kalinin	Amur Yard (Komsomolsk)	39	..4.43	..4.44

Reported as sold (or loaned) to China in about 1952 but this would appear most unlikely.

Name	Builder	Laid down	Launched	Completed
Kaganovich	Amur Yard (Komsomolsk)	39	..10.43	..6.44

Renamed *Petropavlovsk* (1957) and scrapped in the 1960s.

"Frunze" class: **FRUNZE, KUIBISHEV, ORDZHONIKIDZE** (all BS), **CHAPAYEV, CHKALOV, ZHELEZNIAKOV** (all B)

For various reasons the "Kirov" class proved disappointing in service, and they were followed by slightly larger vessels which were lengthened so that an addition triple turret could be worked in aft. To make the main armament more dual-purpose the calibre was reduced to 5·9-inch guns with 50 deg. elevation. The original provision to ship a catapult between the funnels and a triple bank of T.T. on each side was not finally implemented. Compared with the "Kirov" class they had greater freeboard and taller funnels and, with their extra length, were probably better seaboats in consequence.

Displacement:	11,300 tons (15,000 tons full load).
Dimensions:	656 (pp) .... (oa) $\times$ 64 $\times$ 23¾ feet (201·00/.... $\times$ 19·50 $\times$ 7·10 m.).
Machinery:	Six ...... boilers; two shafts; ...... geared turbines S.H.P. 130,000 = 34 knots.
Bunkers and radius:	O.F. 3,500 tons; 7,000 miles @ 20 knots.
Protection:	Generally similar to the "Kirov" class but slightly improved.
Armament:	Twelve 5·9-inch (150 mm.—4 $\times$ 3), eight 3·9-inch A.A. (100 mm.—4 $\times$ 2), twenty-four 37 mm. A.A. (12 $\times$ 2) guns; two hundred mines.
Complement:	840.

The Soviet Navy also projected the construction of several (probably six) large cruisers to be armed with twelve 7·1/8-inch (180/203 mm.) guns. Two were to be built at Leningrad, two at Nikolaiev, and two at the new dockyard at Molotovsk; the latter were laid down in the winter 1940/41, but one was scrapped in 1941 to make room on the building dock for the fitting out of a destroyer and the assembly of submarines, while the second was scrapped after the war. One was laid down at the Annex South of the "Marti" Yard at Nikolaiev after the launch of *Frunze* in early 1941, and two more were laid down at Leningrad during 1940 on the slips vacated by the launching of *Zhelezniakov* and *Chapayev*; these hulls were only about 20% complete when either the German attack or lack of steel forced the Soviets to cancel their construction. The fire-damaged hull of a large unidentified cruiser found by the Germans at the

72

North Annex of the "Marti" Yard had been laid down on the slip vacated by the launch of *Kuibishev*; it was scrapped by them on the slip.

Additional cruiser construction was proposed as a result of the Russo-German pact in 1939 when the Soviet Government asked for the supply of:

(a) 15,000 tons of armour plate, turbines and turbine casings, propeller shafts, condensers, electric motors, and complete armament and fire control equipment to construct four heavy cruisers in Soviet yards;

(b) plans and technical assistance to construct two "Admiral Hipper" class heavy cruisers in Soviet yards; and

(c) to purchase two heavy cruisers of the "Admiral Hipper" class.

However, the German Government would only agree to the sale of one unit—the incomplete *Lützow* which was towed to Leningrad in 1940 where unavailing efforts were made to complete her with the aid of 70 German technical staff. This acquisition was purely political and pushed through by Stalin personally against the advice of his Naval Staff. The Soviet Navy rightly considered that they lacked experience to work the advanced machinery and would be beset with logistic difficulties with regards to spares and ammunition.

Still not complete by the time of the German invasion in 1941 the *Petropavlovsk* (ex-*Lützow*) served only as a floating battery at Leningrad, and was damaged several times by gunfire of German shore batteries and the bombs of German aircraft. She was renamed *Tallin* in 1943, and was never finally completed but served for several years post-war as a training establishment.

A sister vessel—the *Seydlitz*—was found scuttled in Königsberg after the war and was scrapped by the Soviet Navy. Although 95% complete in 1942, this vessel had her armament and superstructure removed by the Germans in 1942–43 and was in the course of conversion into a light aircraft carrier. She was scrapped by the Soviets.

The "Chapayev" class was completed several years after the war. Lower view shows the ZHELEZNIAKOV [JM

Name	Builder	Laid down	Launched	Completed
Kuibishev	Marti North Yard (Nikolaiev)	39	31.1.41	50

Towed incomplete to Poti 6/41 and construction not resumed until 1945.

Frunze	Marti South Yard (Nikolaiev)	39	31.12.40	50

Towed incomplete to Poti 6/41 and stern removed during 1942 to repair damaged cruiser *Molotov*. Construction resumed in 1945, and scrapped in the 1960s.

Ordzhonikidze	Marti South Yard (Nikolaiev)	40	—	—

Captured incomplete at Nikolaiev on 18/8/41 by the Germans and scrapped on slip.

Chapayev	Ordzhonikidze Yard (Leningrad)	38	40	49

Construction suspended 1941–45, and after completion was transferred to the Arctic in 1950 and was scrapped there in 1961.

Zhelezniakov	Marti Yard (Leningrad)	38	40	49

Construction suspended 1941–45, and after completion was transferred to the Arctic in 1950.

Chkalov	Ordzhonikidze Yard (Leningrad)	39	48	50

Construction suspended 1941–45 and renamed *Komsomolets* (1960).

Ex-German "Admiral Hipper" class: **TALLIN** (B)

Displacement:	14,240 tons (18,400 tons full load).
Dimensions:	654½ (pp) 681¼ (oa) × 72 × 21 (26 full load) feet (199·50/207·70 × 21·90 × 6·37/7·94 m)
Machinery:	Twelve Wagner boilers (WP 881 lb/inch.² —60 atü); three shafts; AG Weser geared turbines S.H.P. 132,000 = 32 knots.
Bunkers and radius:	O.F. 3,250 tons; 6,800 miles @ 20 knots.
Protection:	Main belt 2¾–3¾-inch. (70/80 mm.), upper deck ½–2¼-inch (12/30 mm.), main deck 1¼–1¾–2-inch (30/40/50 mm.), turrets 2¾–4-inch (75/105 mm.), fwd C.T. 2–6-inch (50/150 mm.), aft C.T. ¾–1¼-inch (20/30 mm.).
Armament:	(As a floating battery in Soviet naval service) only three 8-inch (203 mm.) and some A.A. guns.
Complement:	?.

Name	Builder	Laid down	Launched	Completed
Tallin (ex-*Petropavlovsk*, ex-German *Lützow*)	AG Weser (Bremen)	37	1.7.39	—

An extremely rare photograph of the incomplete LÜTZOW *being towed to Leningrad in 1940* [*E. Gröner coll.*

FLOTILLA LEADERS

During the First World War the Imperial Navy had conducted some outstandingly successful operations with the (then) large, fast and powerful destroyer *Novik* in the Baltic.

Not surprisingly, the Soviet Navy considered that for raiding operations in the Baltic and Black Sea a type of super-destroyer might again prove useful, and cast a design superior to the German, Swedish, and Turkish destroyers then existing. The Soviet design was clearly inspired by the Italian *esploratori* and French *contre-torpilleurs*, and a certain amount of technical assistance and advice was furnished by French and Italian shipbuilders.

The initial Soviet design—the "Leningrad" class—was not satisfactory, and these vessels proved poor seaboats with many technical shortcomings. After their vulnerability had been demonstrated early in the Second World War, they were thereafter employed cautiously and with reluctance. War modifications included the removal of the amidships 5·1-inch (130 mm.) gun so that the A.A. armament could be augmented.

"Leningrad" class: **BAKU (P/A), KHARKOV (BS), LENINGRAD (B), MINSK (B), MOSKVA (BS), TBILISI (P)**

Displacement:	2,225 tons (2,582 tons full load).
Dimensions:	.... (pp) 418¼ (oa) × 38½ × 13¼ feet (....../127·50 × 11·70 × 4·06 m.).
Machinery:	Three ...... boilers; three shafts; ...... SR geared turbines S.H.P. 66,000 = 36 knots.
Bunkers and radius	O.F. 600 tons; 873/2,100 miles @ 36/20 knots.
Armament:	Five 5·1-inch (130 mm.—5 × 1), two 3-inch A.A. (76 mm.—2 × 1), two 45 mm. A.A. (.. × ..) guns; eight 21-inch (533 mm.—2 × 4—sixteen torpedoes) T.T.; eighty-four type 1926 or sixty-eight type 1931 mines; twenty type B-1 and thirty-two type M-1 DC's.
Complement:	250.

A wartime view of the BAKU

[JM

(Above) *A prewar view of the* LENINGRAD

[*JM/BfZ*

(Right, top) *The* MINSK   [*JM*
(Below) *The* MOSKVA   [*JM/BfZ*

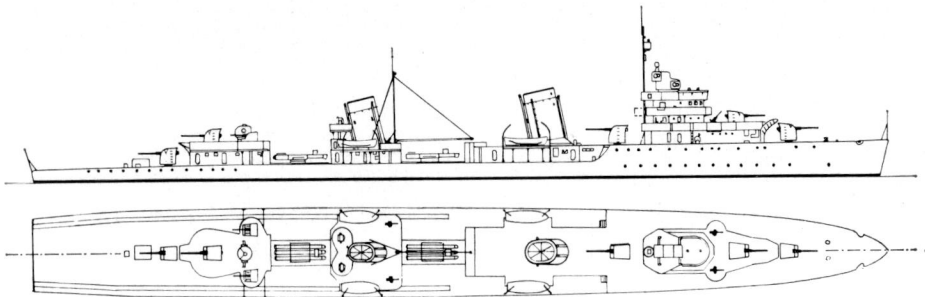

(Above) The "Leningrad" class prewar

[S. Breyer

(Right) The "Leningrad" class as first modified (top) and with final alterations (below). These flotilla leaders were overloaded and not outstandingly successful. Note closeness of "A" gun to the bows [S. Breyer

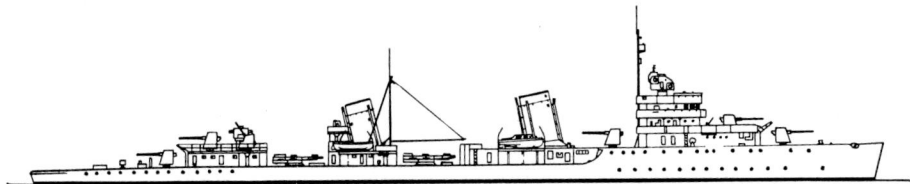

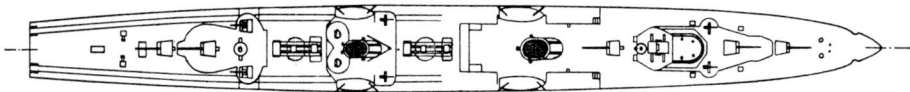

Name	Builder	Built	Fate
Baku (ex-*Ordzhonikidze*)	Komsomolsk Yard	1936/38/39	Transferred from Pacific to Arctic 1942.
Kharkov	Marti South Yard (Nikolaiev)	1936/38/38	Bombed German aircraft off Crimea 6/10/43.
Leningrad	Zhdanov Yard (Leningrad)	1932/33/36	Mined off Tallinn 28/8/41 and repaired; again mined off Hangö 25/11/41 and repaired.
Minsk	—do—	1933/35/39	Mined off Tallinn 28/8/41 and bombed German aircraft 23/9/41 while under repair, salved.
Moskva	Marti South Yard (Nikolaiev)	1935/36/37	Mined off Constanta 26/6/41.
Tbilisi	Komsomolsk Yard	1937/39/40	

Flotilla leader: **TASHKENT** (BS)

Despite a marked hostility to Facist states the Soviet Navy nevertheless placed an order for a flotilla leader in Italy in 1937. Without armament she made 44·2 knots with 116,000 S.H.P. and was delivered in this state in February 1939. When placed in commission three months later the *Tashkent* was provisionally armed with 5·1-inch (130 mm.) guns in single mountings but these were replaced by twin turrets in 1940–41.

For her short period of service the *Tashkent* was mainly mis-employed as a fast transport, and during the siege of Sevastopol she made more than 40 round trips. On her final voyage she made Novorossisk with 1,900 tons of water in her hull, after being bombed by German aircraft off the Crimea on 28/6/42, and foundered. The wreck was partially scrapped by the Germans after Novorossisk was captured, and this was completed by the Soviets when the port was recaptured in 1943. The twin 5·1-inch turrets were salved from the wreck, and two of them were later installed in the destroyer *Ognyevoi* in 1942.

Displacement:	2,893 tons (3,200 tons full load).
Dimensions:	.... (pp) 458½ (oa) × 45 × 12¼ feet (..../139·75 × 13·70 × 3·70 m.).
Machinery:	Two Yarrow boilers; two shafts; ...... SR geared turbines S.H.P. 110,000 = 42 knots.
Bunkers and radius:	O.F. .... tons; ..../4,000 miles @ ../20 knots.
Armament:	Six 5·1-inch (130 mm.—3 × 2), six 45 mm. A.A. (.. × ..), eight 20 mm. A.A. (.. × ..) guns; six 21-inch (533 mm.—2 × 3) T.T.; eighty mines.
Complement:	250.

Name	Builder	Launched	Fate
Tashkent	Odero-Terni-Orlando (Livorno)	21.11.37	Foundered Novorossisk after bombed German aircraft off Crimea 28/6/42, wreck bombed again 2/7/42 and later scrapped.

The Italian-built TASHKENT *was the fastest flotilla leader in the Soviet Navy.*

She was delivered without armament and originally fitted with 5.1-inch guns in single mountings (left) before the twin turrets became available (above) [JM/BfZ]

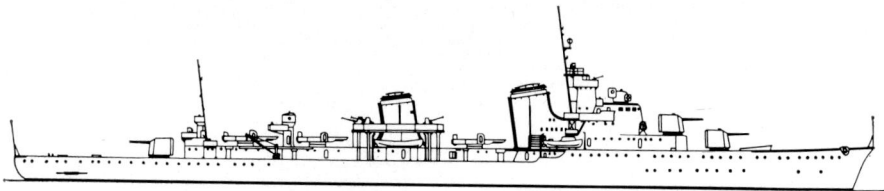

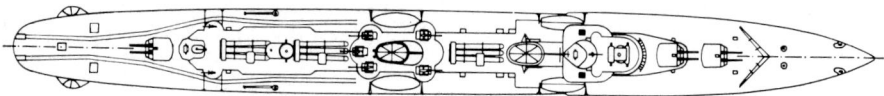

The TASHKENT *with twin turrets*

[S. Breyer

"Kiev" class: **YEREVAN, KIEV, OCHAKOV, PEREKOP** (all BS)

Owing to the indifferent performance of the "Leningrad" class this improved design (B-1) was drawn-up in 1939–40. Only four vessels were actually under construction in June 1941, when the Soviet Union was invaded by Germany, but it is probable that up to sixteen units were to be built (four for each the Arctic, Baltic, Black Sea, and Pacific). Names proposed for projected vessels for the Arctic, *Arkhangelsk, Murmansk*; Baltic—*Kronstadt, Petrozavodsk, Batum, Rostov*; and Pacific—*Volochayevka, Tomsk, Tula, Tver*—cannot be authenticated.

Legend details were displacement about 2,600 tons (3,000 tons full load); a speed of 38 knots with geared turbines; and armament of six 5·1-inch (130 mm.—3 × 2), two 3-inch A.A. (76 mm.—2 × 1), three 45 mm. A.A. (3 × 1), and eight 12·7 mm. A.A. (.. × ..) guns, eight/ten T.T. in two mountings and mines and DC's; and a complement of about 300.

Name	Builder	Built	Fate
Yerevan	Marti South Yard (Nikolaiev)	1939/41/..	Towed incomplete to Khobi River estuary nr. Poti; scrapped after 1945.
Kiev	—do—	1939/40/..	Towed incomplete to Khobi River estuary nr. Poti; scrapped after 1945.
Ochakov	Marti North Yard (Nikolaiev)	1941/../..	Captured incomplete by German Army 18/8/41 and scrapped.
Perekop	—do—	1941/../..	Captured incomplete by German Army 18/8/41 and scrapped.

DESTROYERS

In 1914 the Imperial Navy's *Novik* was the most powerful destroyer in the world, and in the ensuing First World War was frequently employed on offensive minelaying operations. During the war another fifty-three destroyers were ordered based on the prototype *Novik*, but only thirty were completed (seventeen in the Baltic and thirteen in the Black Sea). Of these, three became war losses in 1916–17, twelve were lost, scuttled or captured during the course of the Civil War 1918–20; and six (one incomplete) escaped to Bizerta with White Russian forces and were interned there—and later scrapped by the French; while nine more were cancelled incomplete in WW I. The remaining ten destroyers were still serving in the Soviet Navy after 1920, plus another which had been refloated and recommissioned. Of the fourteen destroyers still incomplete in 1920, six were eventually completed by the Soviet Navy and the others scrapped. Thus, together with the former *Novik*, seventeen old destroyers were still serving in 1941. While all generally similar there were minor differences which divided them into six (type I-VI) sub-groups.

Twelve destroyers were stationed in the Baltic and five in the Black Sea, but in 1933–36 five of the former were transferred to the Arctic from where two were passed into the Pacific via the Northern route.

Destroyer type I: **YAKOV SVERDLOV** (B)

Displacement: 1,271 tons (1,587 tons normal, 1,801 tons full load).

Dimensions: .... (pp) 336 (oa) × 31¼ × 11½ feet (....../102·43 × 9·53 × 3·53 m.).

Machinery: Six Vulkan boilers; three shafts; AEG turbines S.H.P. 36,500 = 36 knots (less than 30 knots by 1941).

Bunkers and radius: O.F. 430 tons; 470/1,800 miles @ 30/16 knots.

Armament: Five 4-inch (102 mm.—5 × 1), one 75 mm. A.A., one 37 mm. A.A. two machine (2 × 1) guns; nine 17·7-inch (450 mm.—3 × 3) T.T.; sixty mines type 1912; five type B-1 and sixteen type M-1 DC's.

Complement: 168.

Name	Builder	Built	Fate
Yakov Sverdlov (ex-*Novik*)	Putilov (St. Petersburg)	1910/11/13	Mined off Moon Island 29/8/41.

Destroyer type II: **FRUNZE** (BS)

Displacement: 1,100 tons (1,300 tons full load).
Dimensions: .... (pp) 305¼ (oa) × 30½ × 9¼ feet (..../93·00 × 9·30 × 2·80 m.).
Machinery: Five Thornycroft boilers; two shafts; Parsons turbines S.H.P. 29,800 = 25 knots.
Bunkers and
radius: O.F. 350 tons; ..../1,800 miles @ ../21 knots.
Armament: Four 4-inch (102 mm.—4 × 1), one 75 mm. A.A., one 37 mm. A.A., two machine (2 × 1) guns; nine 17·7-inch (450 mm.—3 × 3) T.T.; sixty mines.
Complement: 160.

Name	Builder	Built	Fate
Frunze (ex- *Bistry*)	Metal works (Kherson)	1911/14/15	Bombed German aircraft east of Tendra Island 21/9/41.

Note close grouping of guns in the FRUNZE

[PW/JM

Destroyer type III: **KALININ, KARL MARX** (both B)

Displacement:	1,354 tons (1,757 tons normal, 2,200 tons full load).
Dimensions:	.... (pp) 351 (oa) × 31¼ × 16 feet (....../107·00 × 9·50 × 4·90 m.).
Machinery:	Four Normand boilers; two shafts; Parsons turbines S.H.P. 32,700 = 28 knots.
Bunkers and radius:	O.F. 570 tons; 810/1,568 miles @ 27/16 knots.
Armament:	Five 4-inch (102 mm.—5 × 1), one 75 mm. A.A., one 37 mm. A.A., two machine (2 × 1) guns; six 17·7-inch (450 mm.—2 × 3) T.T.; sixty type 1912 or eighty type 1926 mines; sixty type B-1 and twenty type M-1 DC's.
Complement:	168 (+125/180 troops).

Name	Builder	Built	Fate
Kalinin (ex-*Pryemislav*)	Böcker Reval (Tallinn)	1913/15/27	Mined probably off Cape Yuminda 28/8/41.
Karl Marx (ex-*Isiaslav*, ex-*Gromonoset*)	—do—	1913/14/16	Bombed German aircraft Loksa Bight 8/8/41.

The KARL MARX *was the first old destroyer fitted with tripod masts. Note close grouping of guns fore and aft*
[*R. Steen Steensen*

Destroyer type IV: **KARL LIEBKNECHT** (A), **KUIBISHEV** (A), **LENIN** (B), **VOIKOV** (P)

Displacement:	1,260 tons (1,620 tons full load).
Dimensions:	.... (pp) 321½ (oa) × 30¾ × 12¾ feet (..../98·00 × 9·34 × 3·90 m.).
Machinery:	Four Normand boilers; two shafts; AEG turbines S.H.P. 31,500 = 24 knots.
Bunkers and	
radius:	O.F. 500 tons; 634/1,253 miles @ 24/16 knots.
Armament:	Four 4-inch (102 mm.—4 × 1), one 3-inch A.A. (76 mm.), two 45 mm. A.A. (2 × 1), two 37 mm. A.A. (2 × 1), three 13 mm. A.A. (3 × 1), nine machine (9 × 1) guns; nine 17·7-inch (450 mm.—3 × 3) T.T.; sixty type 1912 mines; ten type B-1 and fifteen type M-1 DC's.
Complement:	168 (+100/150 troops). Note: *Kuibishev* had a light tripod mast.

Name	Builder	Built	Fate
Karl Liebknecht (ex-*Kapitan Belli*)	Putilov (St. Petersburg)	1913/15/28	Scrapped postwar.
Kuibishev (ex-*Zhdanov*, ex-*Rykov*, ex-*Kapitan Kern*)	—do—	1913/15/27	Scrapped postwar.
Lenin (ex-*Kapitan Isylmetiev*)	—do—	1913/14/16	Scuttled to avoid capture Libau (Liepaja) 28/6/41.
Voikov (ex-*Trotsky*, ex-*Garibaldi*, ex-*Leitenant Ilin*)	—do—	1913/14/16	Scrapped postwar.

The KARL LIEBKNECHT *shortly before the war* [JM/BfZ]

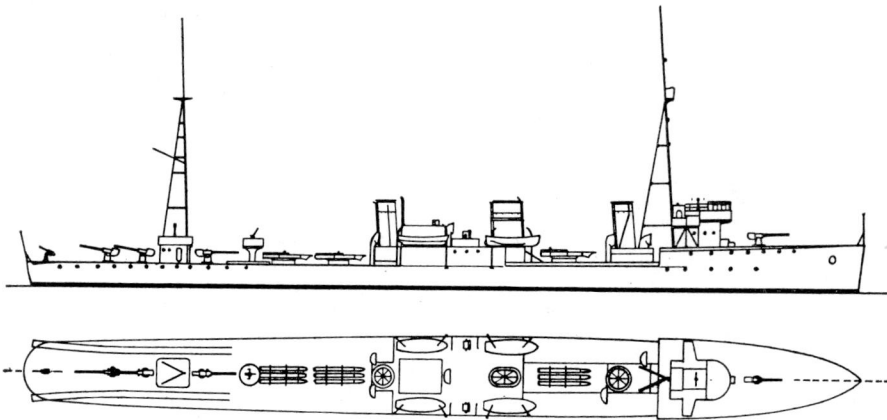

The KUIBISHEV

[S. Breyer

(Above) Wreck of the LENIN *at Libau (Liepaja) in July 1941* [JM/BfZ

(Right, top) Side view of the LENIN *(also* VOIKOV *and* URITZKY*)* [S. Breyer

(Below) The VOIKOV *before the war* [PW/JM

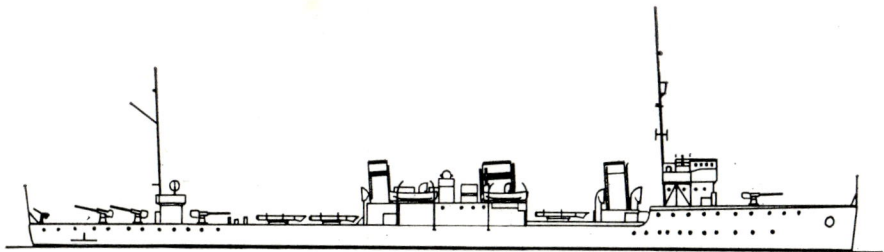

Destroyer type V: **ARTEM** (B), **ENGELS** (B), **STALIN** (P), **URITZKY** (A), **VOLODARSKI** (B)

Displacement:	1,440 tons (1,800 tons full load).
Dimensions:	.... (pp) 321½ (oa) 30½ × 10½ feet (..../98·00 × 9·30 × 3·20 m.).
Machinery:	Four Thornycroft boilers; two shafts; Parsons turbines S.H.P. 32,000 = 24 knots.
Bunkers and radius:	O.F. 500 tons; ..../2,800 @ ../15 knots.
Armament:	Four 4-inch (102 mm.—4 × 1), two 45 mm. A.A. (2 × 1), two 37 mm. A.A. (2 × 1), three 13 mm. A.A. (3 × 1), nine machine (9 × 1) guns; six 17·7-inch (450 mm.—2 × 3) T.T.; sixty mines.
Complement:	160.

Name	Builder	Built	Fate
Artem (ex-*Zinoviev*, ex-*Asard*)	Metal works (St. Petersburg)	1915/16/16	Mined off Cape Yuminda 28/8/41.
Engels (ex-*Desna*)	—do—	1914/15/16	Mined off Cape Yuminda 24/8/41.
Stalin (ex-*Samson*)	—do—	1915/15/16	Scrapped c. 1953.
Uritzky (ex-*Zabiyaka*)	—do—	1914/15/15	Scrapped c. 1953.
Volodarski (ex-*Pobiedityel*)	—do—	1914/15/15	Mined off Seiskari 28/8/41.

(Right, top) The STALIN   [*R. Steen Steensen*
(Below) The VOLODARSKI *carried three guns at the stern* [*JM/BfZ*

Destroyer type VI: **DZERZHINSKY, NYESAMOZHNIK, SHAUMYAN, ZHELEZNIAKOV (all BS)**

Displacement:	1,308 tons (c. 1,700 tons full load).
Dimensions:	.... (pp) 334¾ (oa) × 31¼ × 9¾ feet (...... /102·00 × 9·50 × 3·00 m.).
Machinery:	Five Thornycroft boilers; two shafts; Parsons turbines S.H.P. 32,500 = 26 knots.
Bunkers and radius:	O.F. 390 tons; ..../1,800 miles @ ../20 knots.
Armament:	Four 4-inch (102 mm.—4 × 1), two 45 mm. A.A. (2 × 1), two 37 mm. A.A. (2 × 1), three 13 mm. A.A. (3 × 1), ... machine (. × 1) guns; six 17·7-inch (450 mm.—2 × 3) T.T.
Complement:	160.

Name	Builder	Built	Fate
Dzerzhinsky (ex-*Kaliakria*)	Russian Sbdg. Co. (Nikolaiev)	1915/15/18	Scuttled Novorossisk 18/6/18 by Red Russian forces, salved 1925; recommissioned 1928; mined Sevastopol 14/5/42.
Nyesamozhnik (ex-*Zante*)	—do—	1915/16/23	Scrapped postwar.
Shaumyan (ex-*Levkos*)	—do—	1915/16/25	Bombed and wrecked off Rybachka ../4/42, salved, written-off as constructive total loss and scrapped.
Zhelezniakov (ex-*Petrovsky*, ex-*Korfu*)	—do—	1915/16/25	Handed over Bulgarian Navy 1949; never renamed; exchanged for "Ognevoy" type vessel c. 1956, and scrapped.

(Above) The DZERZHINSKY [*USSR*

(Right) The NYESAMOZHNIK *in 1943* [*USSR*

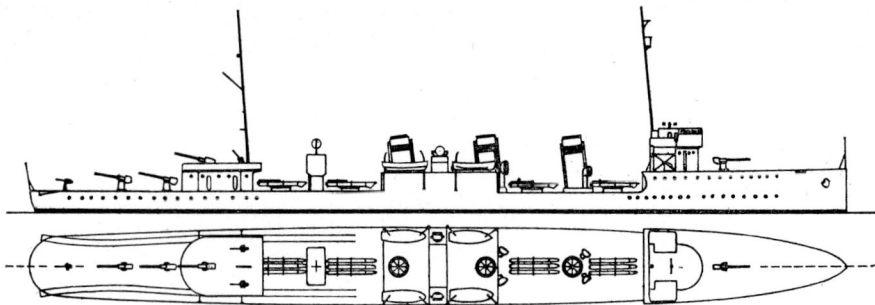

(Above) The NYESAMOZHNIK *prewar* [S. Breyer

(Right) In the SHAUMYAN *the funnels were reduced in height* [PW/JM

Quarter view of the ZHELEZNIAKOV

[*JM/BfZ*

Although the deficiency in Soviet destroyer strength was marked, it was not until the industrial capacity of the country had been restored that any new construction could be undertaken. The type VII destroyer was projected and planned in 1932 with Italian co-operation, but it was not until 1935 that the first unit was laid down.

About nine or ten flotillas (each comprising six destroyers) were contemplated to be distributed between the Baltic (three flotillas), Black Sea (two flotillas), Pacific (three flotillas), and Arctic (one/two flotillas) fleets. The destroyers for the Arctic station were to be built first in the Baltic and later also at Molotovsk in the Arctic; and construction generally was to be spread over two and one-half years per vessel.

After the first twenty-eight units had been ordered the design was modified to suit the more exacting conditions prevalent in the Arctic and the Northern Pacific, and the limited seaworthiness and structural weakness of the type VII was attributed to Italian influence in design. The Soviet Navy therefore produced an improved design, known as the type VII-U (U = *uvelicheniye* = extension) which adopted the unit arrangement of machinery with the boiler and engine rooms alternated. As a result the type VII-U had two funnels, while the type VII had only one as all their boilers were grouped ahead of a common engine room, and the hull was strengthened which permitted a slight increase with installed power. Work on the type VII-U began in 1938 and a total of twenty-six were ordered.

All destroyers of type VII in the Baltic and Black Sea were commissioned by 1941, and ten more had been put in service in the Pacific by 22/6/41. Of the type VII-U only seven vessels were operational in the Baltic and two in the Black Sea. Following the German invasion four more type VII-U were hastily commissioned in the Baltic before trials were completed, to be followed by another two in September 1941. These latter, however, never made open water and throughout the war were employed as floating batteries at Leningrad. In the Black Sea three type VII-U destroyers were commissioned in 1941, one more in the Arctic in 1943, and probably one more of type VII in the Pacific.

Of the fifty-four vessels comprising these two classes one was destroyed in 1941 while under construction at Nikolaiev, another while fitting-out at Sevastopol in 1941; and in the Pacific one was wrecked in tow while still incomplete, and a further five were still under construction when the war ended. The total completed for war service was therefore forty-six of which twenty became war losses but at least one was salved post-war. Destroyers built at Komsomolsk had to be towed incomplete to Sovietskaya Gavan and Vladivostok for fitting-out owing to draught restrictions on the Amur River.

The original class (the VII-U apparently did not have this trouble) was severely handicapped by trouble with turbine machinery and it is probable that some of them were never able to make full speed as a result. In some cases excessive vibration occurred when speed was increased from 150 to 190/200 r.p.m., and irreparable damage at 350 r.p.m. After trials of *Gromky* between 3–7/12/38 the starboard turbine had to be replaced; the *Rezvy* had to reduce to 200/240 r.p.m. the speed of the port turbine during trials on 19/11/39; and similar experiences were shared by *Bystry* and *Steregushchy* in 1939–40 which necessitated replacing damaged turbines. Similar incidents were reported with *Bditelny* and *Bezposhchadny* but with them the damaged turbine blades could be repaired.

In common with all pre-war designs the anti-aircraft armament was found to be inadequate and had to be augmented during the war, but the Soviet Navy was not alone in this respect. Asdic and RDF were not fitted until the close of the war and only after it had been made available from Allied sources; otherwise the type VII normally shipped three rangefinders and three searchlights, and the type VII-U four rangefinders and two searchlights.

Structural failures resulted in the *Gromky* losing her bow and the *Sokrushitelny* foundering due to stress of weather. The *Storozhevoi* was torpedoed by a German MTB in the Irben Straits on 26–27/6/41 and was towed to Leningrad for repair. Here a new bow was fitted and a twin turret replaced the two single 5·1 inch mountings forward. The incomplete *Shchastlivy* was passed from the Baltic to the Arctic in mid-1941 and was completed at Molotovsk. German naval intelligence established her existence by identifying her W/T call sign, her pendant number (06), and the name of her commanding officer but the Soviets have so far never admitted the existence of this vessel by mentioning her name. She was probably lost by unknown cause during 1944 under her new name *Stremitelny* (ii).

A Type VII destroyer in the Arctic [BfZ

Destroyer type VII: **BDITELNY, BEZPOSHCHADNY, BEZUPRECHNY, BODRY, BOIKY, BYSTRY** (all BS), **GNEVNY** (B), **GORDY** (B), **GREMYASHCHY** (A), **GROMKY** (A), **GROZNY** (A), **GROZYASHCHY** (B), **RASTOROPNY, RAZYARYONNY, RAZUMNY, RAZYASHCHY, REKORDNY, RESHITYELNY** (i), **RESHITYELNY** (ii), **RETIVY, REVOSTNY, REZKY, REZVY, RYANY** (all P), **SMETLIVY** (B), **SOKRUSHITELNY,** (A), **STEREGUSHCHY** (B), **STREMITELNY** (A)

Displacement:	1,660 tons (2,039 tons full load).
Dimensions:	.... (pp) 370¼ (oa) × 33½ × 12½ feet (....../112·86 × 10·20 × 3·80 m.).
Machinery:	Three ...... boilers; two shafts; ...... SR geared turbines S.H.P. 48,000 = 38 knots.
Bunkers and radius:	O.F. 540 tons; 800/2,600 miles @ 38/19 knots.
Armament:	Four 5·1-inch (130 mm.—4 × 1), two 3-inch A.A. (76 mm.—2 × 1), four 37 mm. A.A. (.. × ..), one 20 mm. A.A., eight A.A. machine (.. × ..) guns; six 21-inch (533 mm.—2 × 3—twelve torpedoes) T.T.; sixty type 1931 mines; ten/fifteen DC's.
Complement:	197.

(Above) A Type VII destroyer in the Black Sea. This class of destroyers were designed with Italian co-operation but proved deficient in seakeeping qualities in the more exacting Northern conditions JM/BfZ

(Right, top) The Type VII [S. Breyer
(Below) The GORDY *prewar* [JM/BfZ

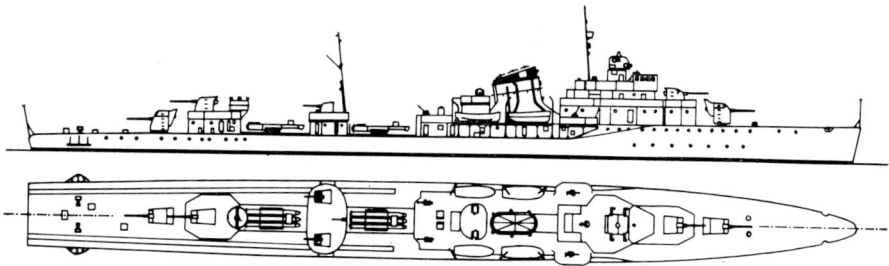

(Above) A wartime view of the GREMYASHCHY

[JM/BfZ]

(Right, top) The SMETLIVY *prewar*   [JM/BfZ]
(Below) The STEREGUSHCHY *postwar*   [JM/BfZ]

The STREMITELNY *with tanker* GORNIAK *prewar*   [*R. Steen Steensen*

Name	Builder	Built	Fate
Bditelny	Marti—North Yard (Nikolaiev)	1937/38/40	Bombed German aircraft Novorossisk 2/7/42 and foundered, reported salved post-war but doubtful.
Bezposhchadny	Sevastopol	1936/37/39	Bombed German aircraft off Crimea 6/10/43.
Bezuprechny	Marti—North Yard (Nikolaiev)	1937/38/39	Bombed German aircraft off Yalta 26/6/42.
Boiky	Marti—South Yard (Nikolaiev)	1937/39/40	Scrapped late 1950s.
Bodry	—do—	1937/38/40	
Bystry	—do—	1937/38/39	German aerial mine Sevastopol 1/7/41 and beached. Later refloated and taken to Kilin Bay where partially scrapped by Germans 6/42.
Gnevny	Zhdanov (Leningrad)	1935/36/39	Mined off Oleg Bank 23/6/41.
Gordy	—do—	1936/37/38	Mined off Naissaari 14/11/41.
Gremyashchy	—do—	1936/37/39	Scrapped late 1950s.
Gromky	—do—	1936/37/39	
Grozny	—do—	1936/37/39	
Grozyashchy	—do—	1936/37/39	
Rastoropny	Komsomolsk	1936/38/40	
Razyaryonny (ex-*Pronzitelny*)	—do—	1937/39/41	Transf. to Arctic 1942.

Name	Builder	Built	Fate
Razumny (ex-*Porazhayushchy?*)	Komsomolsk	1937/39/41	To Arctic 1942.
Razyashchy	Vladivostok	1936/38/41	
Rekordny (ex-*Prozorlivy?*)	Komsomolsk	1938/41/43	
Reshityelny (i)	—do—	1936/38/—	Wrecked incomplete while in tow Komsomolsk/Vladivostok (off Cape Zolotoi) 7/11/38.
Reshityelny (ii) (ex-*Pospeshny?*)	Vladivostok	1938/41/43	
Retivy (ex-*Prytky?*)	Komsomolsk	1939/42/44	
Revnostny	Vladivostok	1937/39/41	
Rezky (ex-*Prochny?*)	—do—	1939/42/44	
Rezvy	—do—	1936/37/40	
Ryany	—do—	1936/37/40	
Smetlivy	Ordzhonikidze (Leningrad)	1937/38/39	Mined and beached Hangö 4/11/41.
Sokrushitelny	—do—	1937/38/39	Foundered Arctic 22/11/42.
Steregushchy	—do—	1937/38/40	Bombed German aircraft off Peterhof 21/9/41, salved post-war.
Stremitelny	—do—	1936/37/39	Bombed German aircraft off Polarnoye 20/7/41.

Grozny was the first vessel to be equipped with SONAR in 1942, to be followed by *Baku* and seven others in 1943 (all in Arctic). *Note:* Three or four of these destroyers in the Pacific were sold to Communist China c. 1955.

A Type VIIU destroyer in the Baltic

[JM/BfZ

Destroyer type VII-U: **SERDITY, STREMITELNY** (ii) (A), **SILNY, SKORY, SLAVNY, SMIELY** (all B), **SMYSHLYONY, SOOBRAZITELNY, SOVERSHENNY, SPOSOBNY** (all BS), **STATNY, STOIKI, STOROZHEVOI, STRASHNY, STROGY, STROINY, SUROVY, SVIREPY** (all B), **SVOBODNY** (BS), and prob. **VNUSHITELNY** (P)

Displacement:	1,686 tons (2,246 tons full load).
Dimensions:	.... (pp) 370¼ (oa) × 33½ × 13¼ feet (...../112·86 × 10·20 × 4·00 m.).
Machinery:	Four ...... boilers; two shafts; ...... SR geared turbines S.H.P. 48,000 (some early units)/54,000 = 36 knots.
Bunkers and radius:	O.F. 500 tons; 625/2,700 miles @ 36/19 knots.
Armament:	Four 5·1-inch (130 mm.—4 × 1), two/three 3-inch A.A. (76 mm.—2/3 × 1), six 37 mm. A.A. (.. × ..), four 13 mm. A.A. (.. × ..) guns; six 21-inch (533 mm.—2 × 3—twelve torpedoes); sixty type 1931 mines; ten/twenty DC's.
Complement:	207.

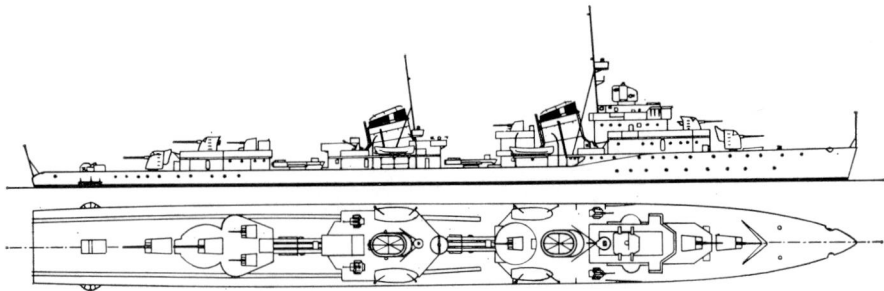

(Above) A Type VIIU ("Silny" group) destroyer in the Baltic postwar [S. Breyer coll.

(Left, top) The SILNY *in 1945. The Type VIIU adopted the unit machinery arrangement which necessitated two funnels, and had better seakeeping qualities than the Type VII* [S. Breyer

(Below) The STOROZHEVOI *with twin turret forward* [S. Breyer coll.

The SVOBODNY *sinking at Korabelnaya Bight, Sevastopol, after bombing by German aircraft in June 1942*
[USSR

Name	Builder	Built	Fate
Serdity	Zhdanov (Leningrad)	1938/39/40	Bombed German aircraft off Oesel (Saaremaa) Island 19/7/41 and scuttled 22/7/41.
Stremitelny (ii) (ex-*Shchastlivy?*)	Ordzhonikidze (Leningrad)	1938/40/43	Completed Molotovsk; torpedoed German submarine *U,997* north of Kola Inlet 5/11/44?
Silny	—do—	1937/39/41	
Slavny	Ordzhonikidze (Leningrad)	1938/39/40	
Skory	Zhdanov (Leningrad)	1938/39/41	Mined off Seiskaari 28/8/41.
Smiely (ex-*Letuchy*)	Ordzhonikidze (Leningrad)	1938/39/40	Probably torpedoed German MTB *S*-54 or mined Gulf of Riga 27/7/41.
Smyshlyony	Marti—North Yard (Nikolaiev)	1938/39/40	Mined off Caucasian coast 20/4/42.
Soobrazitelny	—do—	1938/39/41	
Sovershenny	Sevastopol	1939/40/—	Mined on trials 30/9/41, bombed in dry dock while under repair 12/11/41.
Sposobny	—do—	1939/40/41	Bombed German aircraft off Crimea 6/10/43.
Statny	Zhdanov (Leningrad)	1938/39/41	Mined after damaged by German bombs off Oesel (Saaremaa) Island 18/8/41.
Stoiki (ex-*Likhoi?*)	—do—	1938/39/41	Renamed *Vitse-Admiral Drozd* (1943); scrapped Libau (Liepaja) 1958–59.

Name	Builder	Built	Fate
Storozhevoi	Zhdanov (Leningrad)	1936/38/40	Scrapped Leningrad late 1950s.
Strashny	—do—	1937/39/41	
Strogy	—do—	1938/39/41	
Stroiny	Zhdanov (Leningrad)	1938/39/41	Scrapped Libau (Liepaja) 1958–59.
Surovy (ex-L.....?)	Zhdanov (Leningrad)	1938/39/41	Mined off Hangö 13/11/41
Svirepy	—do—	1938/39/41	
Svobodny	Marti—South Yard (Nikolaiev)	1938/39/41	Bombed German aircraft Korabelnaya Bight (Sevastopol) 10/6/42 and written-off as constructive total loss

Note: Prob. also *Vnushitelny,* prefabricated Nikolaiev 1940, assembled later Komsomolsk (P).

Experimental type: **OPITNY** (B)
This vessel was designed for high speed and completed well before WW II but was not commissioned until late 1941 because trials and experiments had been continuing until June 1941. It did not prove a success owing to the severe vibrations experienced which prevented the guns from being worked. In addition, the lightly built hull could not absorb the stresses when salvoes were fired, so that the *Opitny*'s war service was restricted to a floating battery for the defence of Leningrad.

Name	Builder	Built	Fate
Opitny (ex-*Sergo Ordzhonikidze*)	Zhdanov (Leningrad)	1936/38/41	Scrapped postwar.

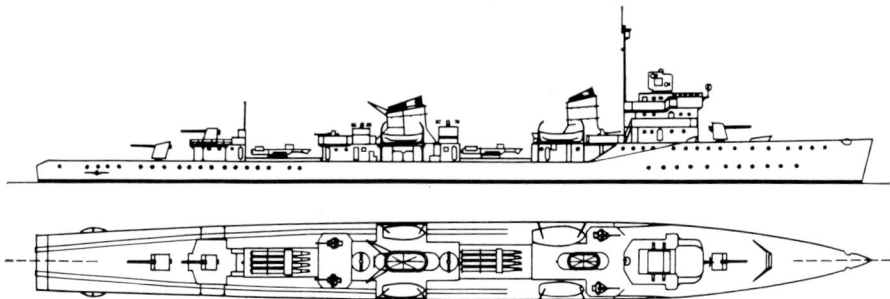

The OPITNY   [S. Breyer

Displacement:	1,670 tons (1,870 tons full load).
Dimensions:	.... (pp) 387¼ (oa) × 38 × 13¾ feet (..../118·00 × 11·60 × 4·20 m.).
Machinery:	Four Ramsin boilers; two shafts; ...... SR geared turbines S.H.P. 70,000 = 42 knots.
Bunkers and	
radius:	O.F. 400 tons; 1,000/3,000 miles @ ../.. knots.
Armament:	Three 5·1-inch (130 mm.—3 × 1), four 45 mm. A.A. (.. × ..), three 37 mm. A.A. (3 × 1) guns; eight 21-inch (533 mm.—2 × 4) T.T.; sixty mines; twenty-five DC's.
Complement:	197/212.

"Ognyevoi" class: **OGNYEVOI, OPASNY, OSORNY, OTVERZHDYONNY** (all BS), **OBRAZTSOVY, ODARYONNY, OSMOTRITELNY, OCHETLIVY, OTLICHNY, OTVAZHNY,** and over **TWENTY** unnamed. Distribution uncertain

Design work on this class, known as *Project 30* was started in 1937 and with a view to securing improved seaworthiness the gun armament was grouped in twin turrets fore and aft. Of at least seventeen vessels of this class two were laid down at Molotovsk in the Arctic, three at Komsomdsk in the Pacific, four in the Black Sea, and eight more at Leningrad. One of these was destroyed incomplete at Nikolaev 1941, and three more building at Leningrad were never completed. Of the remaining vessels eight, or perhaps eleven, were completed post-war while the remainder were cancelled and were scrapped during, or after, the war.

Displacement:	1,800 tons (2,650 tons full load).
Dimensions:	.... (pp) 383¾ (oa) × 38 × 13¾ feet (...... /117·00 × 11·60 × 4·20 m.).
Machinery:	Three ...... boilers; two shafts; ...... SR geared turbines S.H.P. 60,000 = 36 knots.
Bunkers radius:	O.F. ... tons; ..../.... miles @ ../.. knots.
Armament:	Four 5·1-inch (130 mm.—2 × 2), two 85 mm. A.A. (1 × 2), six 37 mm. A.A. (.. × ..) guns; eight 21-inch (533 mm.—2 × 4) T.T.; eighty mines; ...... DC's.
Complement:	250.

(Above) The OGNYEVOI *postwar* [JM

(Left) The OTLICHNY S. Breyer

Name	Builder	Built	Fate
Odaryonny	Zhdanov (Leningrad)	19../../..	Launched (?) and completed post-war.
Ognyevoi	Marti North (Nikolaiev)	1939/41/43	Towed incomplete to Novorossisk, then Poti, and then Batum where completed.
Ozornoi	—do—	1939/41/47	Towed incomplete to Novorossisk, then Poti, then Batum and completed post-war, Bulgarian Navy *Georgi Dimitrov* (c. 1956).
Otverzhdyonny	Sevastopol Naval Yard	1939/41/47	Towed incomplete to Poti, then Batum, and completed post-war.
Osmotritelny	Molotovsk(?)	19../../..	Launched 1944 and completed post-war.
Opasny	Marti North (Nikolaiev)	1939/41/..	Captured incomplete by German Army 16/8/41 and scrapped.
Otchetlivy	Molotovsk(?)	19../../..	Launched and completed post-war.
Otlichny	Zhdanov (Leningrad)	1939/41/47	
Otvazhny	—do—	1939/41/47	
Obraztsovy	—do—	1939/41/47	
Vlastny	Komsomolsk	1940/43/..	
Vnushitelny (?)	—do—	1939/43/..	At least one completed before 8/45.
Vynoslivy	—do—	1940/43/..	
Unnamed	......	1941/../..	
Unnamed	......	1941/../..	
Unnamed	......	1941/../..	Cancelled and scrapped.
Unnamed	......	1941/../..	

LEND-LEASE DESTROYERS

Name	Builder	Launched	Fate
Zharky* (ex-R.N. Brighton, ex-U.S.N. Cowell)	Bethlehem (Fore River)	23.11.18	Retroceded 28/2/49; sold P. W. MacLellan, arrived Bo'ness 5/4/49 for scrapping.
Zhostky* (ex-R.N. Georgetown, ex-U.S.N. Maddox)	—do—	27.10.18	Retroceded 8/9/52; sold T. W. Ward arrived Inverkeithing 16/9/52 for scrapping.
Zhguchi‡ (ex-R.N. Leamington, ex-U.S.N. Twiggs)	New York Sbdg. (Camden)	28.9.18	Retroceded 30/1/50; sold J. Cash more, arrived Newport 26/7/51 for scrapping.
Zhyvuchi (ex-R.N. Richmond, ex-U.S.N. Fairfax)	Mare Island Naval Yard	15.12.17	Retroceded 23/6/49; sold P. W. MacLellan, arrived Bo'ness 12/7/49 for scrapping.
Diatyelny† (ex-R.N. Churchill, ex-U.S.N. Herndon)	Newport News	31.5.19	Torpedoed German submarine U.997 Arctic 16/1/45.
Derzki‡ (ex-R.N. Chelsea, ex-U.S.N. Crowinshield)	Bath I.W.	24.7.19	Retroceded 23/6/49; sold P. W. MacLellan, arrived Bo'ness 12/7/49 for scrapping.
Dostoiny (ex-R.N. St. Albans, ex-U.S.N. Thomas)	Newport News	4.7.18	Retroceded 28/2/49; sold Metal Industries, arrived Charlestown 5/4/49 for scrapping.

Name	Builder	Launched	Fate
Druzhny‡ (ex-R.N. *Lincoln*, ex-U.S.N. *Yarnall*)	Cramp (Philadelphia)	19.6.18	Retroceded 23/8/52; sold Metal Industries, arrived Rosyth ../9/52 for scrapping.
Doblestny* (ex-R.N. *Roxborough*, ex-U.S.N. *Foote*)	Bethlehem (Fore River)	14.12.18	Retroceded 4/2/49; sold Clayton & Davie, arrived Dunston 5/4/49 for scrapping.

The ZHOSTKY *(ex-*R.N. GEORGETOWN, *ex-*U.S.N. MADDOX*) was rearmed for escort work and the A.A. and A/S armament improved*   [*MoD*

Ex-American "Wickes/Clemson" classes: ‡DERZKI, †DIATYELNY, *DOBLESTNY, DOSTOINY, ‡DRUZHNY, *ZHARKY, ‡ZHGUCHI, *ZHOSTKY, ZHYVUCHI (all A)

Displacement:	1,090 tons (1,390 tons full load) except *1,060 tons (1,360 tons full load) and †1,190 tons (1,590 tons full load).
Dimensions:	311 (pp) 314½ (oa) × 31¾ × 8¾ except *8½ and †9¼ feet (94·79/95·86 × 9·68 × 2·66/2·30/2·82 m.).
Machinery:	Four Yarrow except *Zhguchi* Thornycroft, *Derzki* Normand, and *Diatyelny* & *Druzhny* White Foster boilers; two shafts; Curtis except ‡Parsons and †Westinghouse geared turbines S.H.P. 26,000 except *27,000 and *Zhyvuchi* 24,200 = 35 knots.
Bunkers and radius:	O.F. 275 except †375 tons; radius 4,300 except †5,000 miles @ 14 knots.
Armament:	One 4-inch (102 mm.), one 12-pounder A.A. (75 mm.), six 20 mm. A.A. (6 × 1) guns; six 21-inch (533 mm.—2 × 3) T.T.
Complement:	134.

Notes: These vessels were originally armed with four 4-inch (4 × 1) and one 3-inch A.A. guns and twelve 21-inch (4 × 3) T.T. when transferred to the Royal Navy in 1940. Their armament was much reduced to improve A.A. and A/S qualities, and seaworthiness, and sea and air warning radar was added. Eight of these former American destroyers were handed over by the R.N. in the U.K. to the Soviet Arctic Fleet 30/5/44 and reached Polarnoye on 24/8/44. The ninth vessel, *Druzhny*, was handed over 26/8/44 as a "spare parts" ship, but was also commissioned by the Soviet Navy after its arrival 23/9/44.

Up to shortly before the Rumanian surrender the Royal Rumanian Navy had incurred relatively light losses—only two MTBs and some auxiliary vessels—as a result of air attack or mining despite the presence of a far more powerful Soviet Black Sea Fleet.

But on 20/8/44 Constanta was subjected to a particularly heavy Allied air attack, when the torpedo boat *Naluca* was sunk and several other major units damaged, and Rumania capitulated three days later. Constanta was occupied by the Soviet Army on 30/8/44 when all Rumanian warships were seized and incorporated into the Soviet Navy (it would be interesting to find out whether America and Britain claimed their respective shares of the captured tonnage . . .).

These vessels were returned to Rumania in 1949–50, while three submarines were scrapped by the Soviets and one gunboat was probably lost while under Soviet control.

Name	Builder	Launched	Fate
Lovky (ex-R.R.N. *Marasti*, ex-R.It.N. *Nibbio*, ex-R.R.N. *Vartej*)	Pattison (Naples)	19	Renamed *D.11* when retroceded 1949; scrapped 1960s.
Legky (ex-R.R.N. *Marasesti*, ex-R.It.N. *Sparviero*, ex-R.R.N. *Vijelia*)	—do—	18	Renamed *D.12* when retroceded 1949; scrapped 1960s.

The REGELE FERDINAND *in 1944*

[*Nordmark Film. Kiel*

Name	Builder	Launched	Fate
Lyetuchi (ex-R.R.N. *Regina Maria*)	Pattison (Naples)	2.12.28	Retroceded 1953 and renamed *D.22*; changed to *D.10* late 1950s.
Likhoi (ex-R.R.N. *Regele Ferdinand*)	—do—	2.3.29	Retroceded 1953 and renamed *D.21*; changed to *D.9* late 1950s.

Italian type: **LOVKY, LEGKY** (both BS)

This class originally comprised four vessels which were ordered from Italy in 1913 but they were all requisitioned by the Italian Navy on their entry into the First World War. Two of the vessels were subsequently re-purchased by Rumania after the war.

During the Second World War the single 4·7-inch gun amidships was replaced by two 37 mm. A.A. and the 3-inch A.A. guns abaft the funnels by four 20 mm. A.A. (2 × 2) guns.

Displacement:	1,391 tons (1,723 tons full load).
Dimensions:	309½ (pp) .... (oa) × 31 × 11½ feet (94·33/.... × 9·45 × 3·51 m.).
Machinery:	Five Thornycroft boilers; two shafts; Tosi geared turbines S.H.P. 44,000 = 34 knots.
Bunkers and radius:	O.F. 260 tons; 1,700 miles @ 15 knots.
Armament:	Five 4·7-inch (120 mm.—2 × 2 and 1 × 1), two 3-inch A.A. (76 mm.—2 × 1), two machine A.A. (2 × 1) guns; four 17·7-inch (450 mm.—2 × 2) T.T.; fifty mines.
Complement:	139.

Thornycroft type: **LYETUCHI, LIKHOI** (both BS)

These vessels were modelled on the "Shakespeare" class flotilla leaders designed and built for the Royal Navy by Thornycroft during the First World War.

Displacement:	1,821 tons (2,320 tons full load).
Dimensions:	.... (pp) 334½ (oa) × 31½ × 11½ feet (...... /101·95 × 9·60 × 3·51 m.).
Machinery:	Four Thornycroft boilers; two shafts; Parsons geared turbines S.H.P. 48,000 = 35 knots.
Bunkers and radius:	O.F. 480 tons; 3,000 miles @ 18 knots.
Armament:	Five 4·7-inch (120 mm.—5 × 1), one 3-inch A.A. (76 mm.), two 2-pounder A.A. (40 mm.—2 × 1) guns; six 21-inch (533 mm.—2 × 3) T.T.; fifty mines.
Complement:	212.

TORPEDO BOATS

Of ninety-five torpedo boats over 200 tons in service with the Imperial Navy in 1914, twelve were lost during WW I and another forty-seven during the Civil War. About thirty-six torpedo boats served in 1920 with the GPU (later NKVD) units and the Soviet Navy (mainly as training ships)—but only very few remained in service in 1939: one in the Baltic, one on Lake Ladoga, and three in the Caspian Sea.

Schichau type: **MARTYNOV** (B)

After a refit in 1940 this craft was used for training purposes by the Naval Academy at Leningrad. She was subsequently transferred to Lake Ladoga and was scrapped during, or soon after, the war.

Displacement:	350 tons.
Dimensions:	$208\frac{3}{4}$ (pp) .... (oa) $\times$ 22 $\times$ 5 feet (63·60/.... $\times$ 6·70 $\times$ 1·50 m.).
Machinery:	Four ...... boilers; two shafts; reciprocating (VTE) I.H.P. 6,200 = 20 knots.
Bunkers and radius:	Coal 95 tons; .... miles @ .. knots.
Armament:	Two 75 mm. (2 $\times$ 1), four machine (4 $\times$ 1) guns; three 17·7-inch (450 mm.—1 fixed bow and 2 $\times$ 1).
Complement:	64.

Name	Builder	Launched	Fate
Martynov (ex-*Vnouchitelny*)	Schichau (Elbing)	05	Scrapped 1940s.

"Shtorm" class: **BURYA** (B), **BURUN** (P), **GROM** (P), **GROZA** (A), **MYETEL** (P), **MOLNYA** (P), **PURGA** (B), **SHKVAL** (BS), **SHTORM** (BS), **SMERCH** (A), **SNIEG** (B), **TAIFUN** (B), **TUCHA** (B), **URAGAN** (A) **VIKHR** (B), **VYUGA** (P), (A), **ZARNITSA** (P), **ZYKLON** (B)

Owing to the poor material condition of the few surviving Tsarist-built torpedo boats the Soviet Navy decided to replace them in 1928 with a new series of craft for local patrol work which were classed as guard ships (*storozhevoi korably*) and not as torpedo boats.

As these were the first surface warships to be built by Soviet yards they not unnaturally possessed many shortcomings. Their construction was generally poor, their stability was suspect, and with inexperienced engine room personnel none made their contract speed of 29 knots. They were not an identical series of vessels but comprised the "Shtorm", "Taifun", and "Uragan" sub-groups, and were too slow to act as torpedo boats and were of little use as escorts owing to lack of A/S equipment.

The *Burun*, *Grom*, *Myetel* and *Vyuga*, built in the Baltic, were dismantled for shipment and reassembled at Vladivostok 1936–37, and most of the material of the two other units launched in the Far East was manufactured in the Western part of the U.S.S.R. Originally old 4-inch/60 cal. (102 mm.) low angle guns with a slow rate of fire were mounted, but during the war some of the surviving vessels were probably armed with the new 3·9-inch/51 cal. (100 mm.) gun developed in the 1930s. It is also probably that the A.A. armament was augmented during the war and the T.T. removed in 1942.

(Right, top) The TUCHA   *S. Breyer*

(Below) "Taifun" group torpedo boats in the Baltic. Note the gun shields and other details different from the TUCHA   [*S. Breyer coll.*

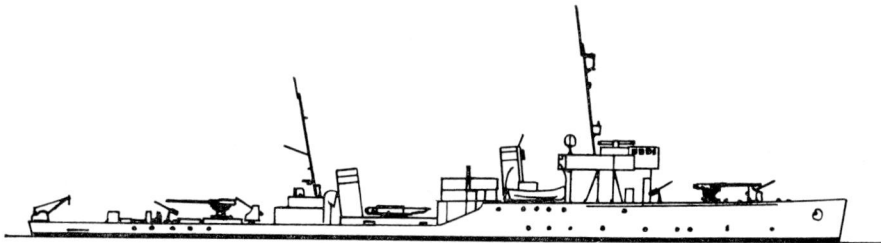

"Taifun" group (B)

Displacement: .. tons (580 tons full load).
Dimensions: 487 (pp) 233 (oa) × 24¼ × 9¼ feet (..../71·00 × 7·40 × 2·80 m.).
Machinery: Two ...... boilers; two shafts; ...... geared turbines S.H.P. 6,440 = 25 knots.
Bunkers and
radius: O.F. 115 tons; 1,400 miles @ .. knots.
Armament: Two 3·9-inch A.A. (100 mm.) (2 × 1), two 37 mm. (2 × 1) guns; four machine (.. × ..) guns; three 17·7-inch (450 mm.—1 × 3) T.T.; twenty-four mines, fifty DC's.
Complement: 101.

"Uragan" group (A)

Displacement: .... tons (635 tons full load).
Dimensions: .... (pp) 236¼ (oa) × 24¾ × 9½ feet (..../72·00 × 7·50 × 2·90 m.).
Machinery: Two ...... boilers; two shafts; ...... geared turbines S.H.P. 6,200 = 25 knots.
Bunkers and
radius: 125 tons; 1,400 miles @ .. knots.
Armament: Two 3·9-inch (100 mm.) (2 × 1), four 45 mm. A.A. (.. × ..), two machine (2 × 1) guns; three 17·7-inch (450 mm.—1 × 3) T.T.; twenty four mines, fifty DC's.
Complement: 88.

"Shtorm" group (BS)

Displacement: 487 tons (560 tons full load).
Dimensions: .... (pp) 234½ (oa) × 24¼ × 9¼ feet (..../71·50 × 7·40 × 2·80 m.).
Machinery: Two ...... boilers; two shafts; ...... geared turbines S.H.P. 5,000 = 24 knots.
Bunkers and
radius: O.F. 120 tons; 1,400 miles @ .. knots.
Armament: Two 4-inch (102 mm.—2 × 1), four 45 mm. and one 37 mm. guns; three 17·7-inch (450 mm.—1 × 3) T.T., twenty-four type 1912 mines, twenty type B-1 and thirty type M-1 DC's.
Complement: 90.

A unit of the "Shtorm" class. These vessels were of poor construction and design and too slow to act as torpedo boats
[JM

Pt. No.	Name	Builder	Launched	Fate
S.1	Shtorm	Marti Yard (Nikolaiev)	..7.29	Scrapped post-war.
S.5	Shkval	—do—	30	Scrapped post-war.
S.2	Taifun	Zhdanov Yard (Leningrad)	..7.29	Bombed German aircraft Kronstadt 23/9/41, but repaired.
S.3	Vikhr	—do—	29	Hulked and subsequently scrapped Leningrad after heavy bomb damage 23/9/41.
S.4	Zyklon	—do—	30	Mined off Cape Yuminda 28/8/41.
S.6	Groza	—do—	30	Scrapped c. 1959.
S.7	Myetel	—do—	30	Scrapped c. 1959.
S.8	Smerch	—do—	31	DOSAAF training vessel 1950s; scrapped c. 1959.
S.9	Uragan	—do—	31	
S.10	Vyuga	—do—	31	scrapped c. 1959.
S.11	Purga	—do—	32	Bombed German aircraft Lake Ladoga 1/9/42, salved (?).
S.12	Burya	—do—	32	Mined E. of Lavansaari Is. 27/8/42.
S.13	Grom	—do—	32	Scrapped ?
S.14	Snieg	—do—	33	Mined off Cape Yuminda 28/8/41.
S.15	Tucha	—do—	34	} Scrapped ?
S.16	Burun	—do—	34	
S.17	Molnya	Voroshilov Yard (Vladivostok)	35	} Scrapped ?
S.18	Zarnitsa	—do—	35	

"Yastreb" class: **BERKUT, GRYF, KONDOR, KORSHUN, ORYOL, VORON, YASTREB,** and **ONE** unnamed (all B)

A second series of ships—the "Bird" (or "Ptitsi") class—were laid down between 1939–41, and comprised the "Yastreb" and "Albatros" sub-groups each of eight vessels.

With the 2-funnelled "Yastreb" group one gun and the triple bank of T.T. had to be sacrificed to reduce topweight, but the armament was not reduced in the "Albatros" sub-group although the installed power was practically halved. Basically there was no difference between these two groups: both were 2-funnelled types and the machinery was identical. However, because of wartime demands and shortages there were some differences in armament. After the war one 100 mm. gun was removed from some units.

According to German intelligence sources at least four of the "Yastreb" group were afloat by 1941, three of which were completed between 1942–44, although there is no information yet just how many of this class were finally completed.

Displacement: 840 tons (1,250 tons full load).
Dimensions: .... (pp) 275½ (oa) × 27¼ × 9¾ feet (..../84·00 × 8·30 × 3·00 m.).
Machinery: Four ...... boilers; two shafts; ...... geared turbines S.H.P. 23,000 = 30 knots.
Armament: Three 3·9-inch A.A. (100 mm.—3 × 1), four 37 mm. A.A. (.. × ..) guns, eight machine guns; twenty mines, Two DC mortars.
Complement: 48.

(Top) The "Ptitsi" ("Bird") class as built
(Lower) The "Ptitsi" ("Bird") class as modified

[S. Breyer

(Above and following page) A "Ptitsi" class torpedo boat in the Baltic postwar   S. Breyer coll.

Name	Builder	Built	Fate
Yastreb	Zhdanov Yard (Leningrad)	1939/40/41	Scrapped Libau (Liepaja) c. 1959.
Oryol	Russki Diesel Works (Leningrad)	1940/41/42	
Korshun	—do—	1940/41/42(?)	
Berkut	Two launched by Zhdanov Yard 1941, another on slipway same Yard; one at Izhora Yard, Leningrad		Not known if completed or not.
Gryf			
Kondor			
Voron			

"Albatros" class: **ALBATROS, CHAIKA, KRECHET** (P), and **FIVE** unnamed vessels (prob. BS)

Of this group only *Albatros* is known to have been commissioned in 1944. However, because no 100 mm. guns were available then in the Pacific area, she was originally fitted with three 3·5-inch (85 mm.) from an incomplete unidentified warship. Also no 37 mm. A.A. guns were available and the remaining armamant of the *Albatros* in 1944/45 was limited to four machine guns and three 17·7-inch (450 mm.) T.T.s. In addition, *Albatros* was originally commissioned with only two of her boilers operational and therefore could develop only 12,300 S.H.P. It is probable that *Albatros* received her full armament/equipment post-war. At present it is not known whether or not *Chaika* and *Krechet* were ever completed or scrapped. The other five units were laid down in Nikolaiev during 1940–41 and their incomplete hulls fell practically undamaged into German hands when they captured the port in 1941. However, as all plans had been destroyed their completion presented a problem and they were therefore scrapped on the slip. It is however possible that these hulls were of "Polukhin" class minesweepers.

Displacement: 920 tons (. . . . tons full load).
Dimensions: . . . . (pp) 279 (oa) × 27½ × 9¾ feet (. . . ./85·00 × 8·40 × 3·00 m.).
Machinery: Two . . . . . . boilers; two shafts; . . . . . . geared turbines S.H.P. 12,300 = 25 knots.
Armament: Three 3·9-inch A.A. (100 mm.—3 × 1), six 37 mm. A.A. (. . × . .), eight machine (. . × . .) guns; three 21-inch (533 mm.—1 × 3) T.T.; twenty mines.
Complement: 92.

Name	Builder	Built	Fate
Albatros	Far East ?	../41/44	
Krechet	—do—	../41/—	
Chaika	—do—	../41/—	
FIVE unnamed	Marti (North) Yard (Nikolaiev)	—	Captured incomplete by Germans and scrapped on slip.

According to official Soviet sources there were nine escort vessels in the Pacific Fleet at the beginning of 1945, against only six in mid-1941. These latter were the guard ships of the "Uragan" group; and Allied intelligence reported that two more escort vessels were completed during the war, probably belonging to the "Bird" class.

Following the surrender of Rumania and Bulgaria in 1944 the Soviet Black Sea Fleet took over a total of six old and small torpedo boats which they used for minesweeping.

Ex-Rumanian type: **TWO** vessels (names not known) (all BS)
These former Austro-Hungarian torpedo boats were ceded to Rumania after the First World War. During the Second World War they were modified for escort work when the two twin banks of T.T. were removed and they were re-armed with modern guns. A third unit—the *Nalucu*—was lost by air attack.

Displacement:	262 tons.
Dimensions:	187 (pp) .. (oa) × 18¾ × 5 feet (57·00/.... × 5·70 × 1·50 m.).
Machinery:	Two Yarrow boilers; two shafts; ...... turbines S.H.P. 5,000 = 24 knots.
Bunkers and radius:	O.F. 24/34 tons + coal 18/20 tons; .. miles @ .. knots.
Armament:	Two 3·5-inch A.A. (88 mm.—2 × 1), two 20 mm. A.A. (2 × 1) guns; ...... DC's.
Complement:	30

Name	Builder	Launched	Fate
...... (ex-R.R.N. *Smeul*, ex-Austro-Hungarian *T*.83)	Ganz-Danubius (Fiume)	14	Retroceded 1949 and scrapped late 1950s.
...... (ex-R.R.N. *Sborul*, ex-Austro-Hungarian *T*.81)	Stab. Tecnico (Trieste)	14	Retroceded 1949 and scrapped late 1950s.

(Above) The SMEUL in 1944

(Left) The SBORUL in 1944.

[Nordmark Film, Kiel

Ex-Bulgarian type: **FOUR** vessels (names not known) (BS)

Displacement:	97 tons (.. tons full load).
Dimensions:	124¾ (pp) .. (oa) × 14½ × 8½ feet (38·00/.... × 4·40 × 2·60 m.).
Machinery:	Two Guyot boilers; one shaft; reciprocating (VTE) I.H.P. 2,000 = 15 knots.
Bunkers and radius:	Coal 11 tons; 1,800 miles @ 10 knots.
Armament:	Two 47 mm. (2 × 1), one machine guns; two 17·7-inch (450 mm.—1 × 2) T.T.
Complement:	32.

Name	Builder	Built	Fate
. . . . . . (ex-Bulgarian *Derski*)	Ch. Schneider-Creusot (. . . . . .)	1907–08	Retroceded 1947 and hulked as naval museum Varna (1955).
. . . . . (ex-Bulgarian *Hrabri*)	—do—	1907–08	Retroceded 1947 and scrapped 1952–55.
. . . . . (ex-Bulgarian *Smely*)	—do—	1907–08	Retroceded 1947 and scrapped 1952–55.
. . . . . (ex-Bulgarian *Strogi*)	—do—	1907–08	Retroceded 1947 and scrapped 1952–55.

(Left) The old DERSKI *is now preserved as a naval relic at Varna, Bulgaria* [*JR*

CONTENTS

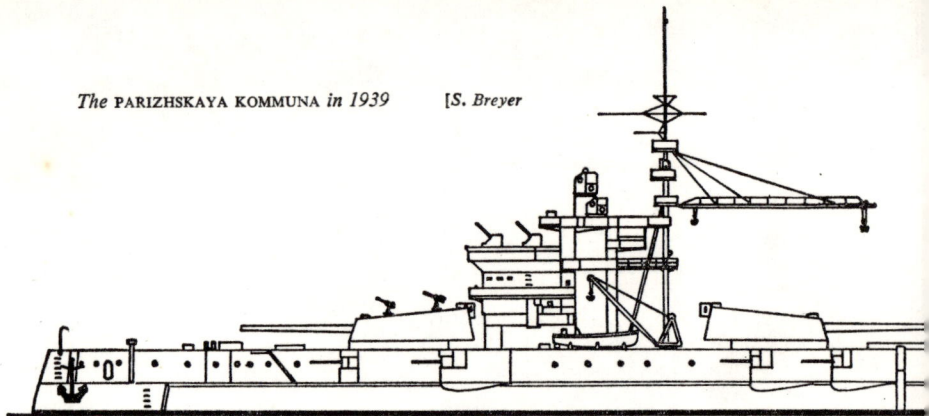

The PARIZHSKAYA KOMMUNA *in 1939* [S. Breyer

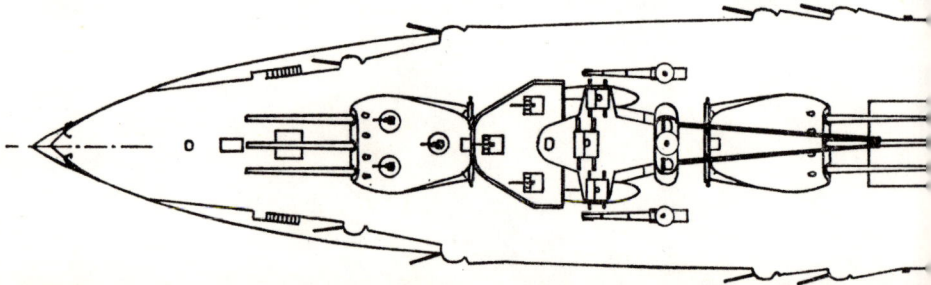